Anyone wondering if there is more to life than what they are experiencing should get this book. Love Is the Foundation: Unlock the Healing Power of Love and Rediscover Your True Self explains how you can tap the power of your inner consciousness to overcome unproductive patterns of behavior and learn how to live your best life. Author A'sha Love has written a remarkable instruction manual for getting in touch with your inner self and discovering how to be your best self.

Tamara Nall | CEO & Founder, The Leading Niche

One of the best books about personal transformation I have ever read. A'sha Love expertly delineates how people are often conditioned to behave and believe in ways that don't correspond to their true selves and how they can overcome this to be who they truly are—not what someone else wants them to be. The book provides both a multidimensional theoretical framework for understanding this dynamic and practical tips for rising about it. Truly an indispensable resource for anyone looking to restructure their consciousness in order to live their best life.

Sanjay Jaybhay | Author of Invest and Grow Rich

Modern science is coupled with ancient wisdom about the power of our thoughts in this groundbreaking book by consciousness expert A'sha Love. In the book, she explains how changing the way we think can enable us to achieve a personal transformation in who we are and how we relate to the world. Engrossing throughout, Love Is the Foundation: Unlock the Healing Power of Love and Rediscover Your True Self is a must-read for anyone looking for a way to improve their ability to become their most authentic self.

David Fuess | CEO, Henson Group

Anyone looking to transcend the limitations imposed on them by other people's expectations should read this book. A'sha Love brilliantly details the benefits people can realize from freeing their consciousness from ideas driven by agendas other than their own. She persuasively explains how finding what it is a person truly desires frees them to live their best life.

Shawn Johal | Business Growth Coach, Elevation Leaders, Bestselling Author of The Happy Leader

Many people go through life thinking and doing things the way others have taught them. To help them break free of this conditioning, consciousness and personal transformation expert A'sha Love has written a book that contains a wealth of ideas and techniques for thinking multidimensionally in order to take charge of your life. Anyone looking to embark on a personal journey that taps into the capacity of their consciousness to transform their perspective and improve their ability to be who they want to be can benefit from reading this book.

**Dr. Kathy Humel | CEO,
Senior Consultant RxKHumel, LLC**

LOVE
IS THE
FOUNDATION

Unlock the Healing Power of Love
&
Rediscover Your True Self

BY A'SHA LOVE

Copyright © 2023 A'sha Love
Published in the United States by Story Leaders.
www.leaderspress.com

All rights reserved. No part of this book may be reproduced or transmitted in any form or by any means, electronic or mechanical, including photocopying, recording, or by an information storage and retrieval system – except by a reviewer who may quote brief passages in a review to be printed in a magazine or newspaper – without permission in writing from the publisher.

All trademarks, service marks, trade names, product names, and logos appearing in this publication are the property of their respective owners.

ISBN 978-1-63735-198-7 (hcv)
ISBN 978-1-63735-197-0 (pbk)
ISBN 978-1-63735-199-4 (ebook)

Library of Congress Control Number: 2023916107

DEDICATION

This book is dedicated to all the remarkable souls who can't help but feel that persistent inner nudge, like a friendly cosmic reminder that something incredible awaits. To each of you, the seekers, the dreamers, the explorers of the heart's deepest mysteries, "Love Is the Foundation" is a heartfelt compass for your exhilarating journey. With boundless love, laughter, and the promise of limitless potential, I salute you all. Here's to your magnificent quest! In Unity, A'sha Love

CONTENTS

Introduction: Unleash Your Inner Adventurer 1

Chapter One: Be Your Own Guru 5

Chapter Two: The Law of Vibration 15

Chapter Three: Trust Your Intuition 25

Chapter Four: Meet Your Inner Skeptic and Critic 31

Chapter Five: Mindfulness is the Foundation 39

Chapter Six: The Positive Use of Free Will 45

Chapter Seven: The Law of Attraction 51

Chapter Eight: What's Your Story? 59

Chapter Nine: The Importance of Psychic Hygiene 73

Chapter Ten: Self-Sovereignty 83

Chapter Eleven: Setting Healthy Boundaries 93

Chapter Twelve: Create Your Future 101

Chapter Thirteen: What's Your Soul Purpose? 109

Chapter Fourteen: Surrender 115

Introduction

UNLEASH YOUR INNER ADVENTURER

Welcome, my fellow adventurers, to a quest like no other—a multidimensional journey, where love reigns supreme and fear is left trembling in its wake. Are you ready to embark on this thrilling expedition of self-discovery and remembrance? Then buckle up!

For the past fifteen years, I've navigated a metaphysical awakening, immersing myself in the wondrous world of the multidimensional ecosystem in which we live. Amazingly, as I finish this book in the summer of 2023, the world is becoming acquainted with the fact that there is, indeed, something more to reality than we've been led to believe.

Picture this: we're standing with one foot in the known and the other in the unknown—a cosmic balancing act. This book is here to bridge the gap and guide you toward the deeper truths that lie just beyond the veil of conventionality.

Now, let's get real for a moment. I used to be a skeptic too, brushing off anything metaphysical as hogwash. But, oh, how the tides have turned! Throughout my own awakening, I've encountered remarkable souls—intelligent, curious beings like yourself—who long for a profound understanding of life and an inkling that there's something grander at play.

Consider this book your personal invitation to dive headfirst into a greater version of self that resides within each and every one of us. It's my heartfelt hope that these pages will challenge and expand your worldview, propelling you toward a life filled with authenticity and boundless joy. Together, we'll find our way back home to love as the foundation.

The other day, the universe whispered a clear message into my ear, revealing my purpose on this planet: to guide people back from the illusion of separation that causes so much unnecessary suffering. So, I'm extending an invitation that I hope will awaken the explorer within you.

Now, fair warning, my fellow adventurers—this journey won't always be a walk in the park. We'll encounter layers of conditioning imprinted on our subconscious from childhood, like a tangled mess of old Christmas lights.

Let me give it to you straight—this book might rock your world and open you up to experiences that challenge everything you thought you knew. You see, I believe the time is ripe for exploration. When I began my own awakening fifteen years ago, the idea of multidimensional reality was met with raised eyebrows. Yet society has come a long way since then, opening doors to new possibilities and expanded perspectives.

Throughout my career, I've had the privilege of working with an incredible mix of individuals from all walks of life. They may have diverse backgrounds, but they share a common hunger—to answer the inner call to something greater within, unlock more of their potential, and make this world a more harmonious place to live in.

They recognize that life is about more than just going through the motions—it's about diving headfirst into the deliciously deep pool of existence.

This book isn't here to hand you all the answers on a silver platter. No. It's here to ignite a fire within you, a fire that will drive you to seek truth for yourself, to become the guru of your own life. But hold on tight, because we've got some barriers to break through before we can bask in that clarity.

To all you curious souls and open-minded explorers out there, this book is for you. It's for those willing to break free from the chains of conventional reality and embrace the mind-bending vastness that lies just beyond the edge of what we've been taught. Trust me, fear may have snuck its way into your life, obscuring your true voice and power. But, together, we'll shine a light on that darkness and reclaim our fearless pursuit of our greater purpose.

As we peel back the layers of conditioning, we'll envision lives bursting with purpose and joy. Picture a reality where time, money, resources, fear of judgment—none of it holds you back. What would you do? Most people don't even ask themselves this question. They're too busy running on autopilot, guided by cultural programming that focuses our attention on just a fraction of reality. But guess what? We're about to break free from that trap.

The good news is that the fear-based foundations we've built our lives upon are crumbling as we speak. They can't stand the test of time any longer. And you know what? That's a good thing! Because true growth lies not in control and staying within our comfort zone, but in having faith, trusting in something greater than our fears. So, let's shake off those shackles and embark on this adventure of a lifetime!

Think of this book as your trusty how-to handbook, your guiding light as we navigate the choppy waters of letting go who you thought you had to be so you can be who you were all along. My sincerest wish is for you to discover that your life raft lies within, that you hold the power to save yourself. We are the heroes of our own stories and, together, we'll evolve to new heights of human experience.

So, if you're ready to bid farewell to those reductionist worldviews and embrace a life that's overflowing with meaning and magic, then you've come to the right place. Get ready, because a transformative journey awaits, and the answers you seek lie within, patiently waiting to be revealed.

A'sha Love
August 2023

P.S. Want to get a jump on the self-liberation part of this journey? Then it's time to embrace your psychic hygiene! Begin by picking up my Daily Grounding and Clearing Meditation by visiting my website and clicking on "Gift Meditation": www.multidimensionalu.com.

Chapter One
BE YOUR OWN GURU

Ever notice how we've been conditioned to chase after the right answer, desperately seeking approval? It's like an invisible leash tied around our necks, starting from the moment we set foot in school. And the crazy part? We often don't even realize how deeply ingrained it is!

I'm here to flip the script and invite you on a wild adventure of self-discovery. You are going to be your very own guru, my friend. No, I won't be dictating what you should do or how you should think. Instead, we're diving deep into the inner self, where the real treasure lies.

Say goodbye to living life on someone else's terms. It's time to tap into your wellspring of wisdom from within. And guess what? Love, not fear, is your birthright. So let's rebuild your life on a foundation of love, shall we?

Let's pause for a moment and ponder the mind-blowing notion of a vast reality that we've forgotten along the way, but are ready to remember. It's time to break free from the shackles of conditioning and embrace the truth of who you truly are—an incredible multidimensional being!

What does that mean exactly? It means you have vast, untapped resources within you. Now, here's the secret: you are a creator extraordinaire! Believe it or not, you have more power in shaping your reality than all the superheroes combined. And guess what? It all starts with setting intentions.

Feeling free and on purpose is your birthright, but it won't come knocking on your door with a shiny bow. Nope, you gotta claim it. So, let's answer the inner call to something greater by setting those intentions. How do you want to live your life? How do you want to feel when you reach the end of this epic journey called life? Start by setting your intentions each morning detailing what kind of day you'd like to create. Journal it out in detail, with lots of joy and positive emotion!

I don't know about you but, when I look back on my life, I want an ear-to-ear grin on my face. I wanna high-five the universe, knowing I unleashed my inner adventurer and embraced every darn thing my soul came here to experience and create. No holding back!

Transforming Your Relationship with Reality

Reality isn't some rigid, separate thing that's out there, beyond our grasp. Nope, that's not how the universe works. Reality is like an ever-evolving field of flexible material that we can mold from the inside out. How cool is that?

When we shift our consciousness and shake up our beliefs, we're flexing our free-will muscles and literally reshaping the world around us. It's like being the master chefs of our own reality kitchen.

Our subconscious mind is a wild cocktail of influences—cultural conditioning, ancestral memories, trauma, and even stuff from other dimensions and past lives. And if we want to whip up a reality that suits our taste buds, we must address these hidden ingredients.

Ever found yourself caught in a loop of doom and gloom, wondering why life keeps throwing the same stuff your way? Well, my fellow reality benders, it's time for some inner spelunking. We're gonna dive deep and unravel the dysfunctional patterns and negative beliefs that keep tripping us up. Say goodbye to victimhood, 'cause you're in the driver's seat now!

Just because we've grown accustomed to feeling a certain way doesn't mean we're stuck with it. Life's a buffet, and we can make fresh choices every single day. It's time to swing open the doors of possibility, jump on a new cosmic rollercoaster, and invite joy and happiness into our lives.

The way we approach one thing reflects how we approach everything. If we're cruising through life grumpy, exhausted, and ready to pull our hair out, guess what? We're waving a big ol' flag to the universe, saying, "Bring me more of this nonsense!" But if we flip the switch and embrace a lighter and happier vibe, get ready for a wild ride of greater abundance and fulfillment.

Your Mindset: Embrace the Adventure Within

If you're looking around and thinking "Is this all there is?", then this book is your ticket to discovering that there's a whole lot more in store for you. But hold on, because the treasure you seek isn't out there in the world—it's right here, within you. We're going on an epic inner journey, and let me tell you, it's not always a walk in the park. We've all had moments when we closed off our hearts, but it's time to open them wide again.

To embark on this adventure, we need to be open-minded, open-hearted, and ready to rock the boat. Let's admit it—sometimes we're a bit too arrogantly ignorant. But, as we wake up to a greater reality and the mind-blowing laws of multidimensional physics, we gotta leave our egos at the door. Trust me, it's a humbling experience.

Here's the deal: we need to give our inner skeptic a vacation and consider that it might not be as helpful as we think. That little voice of doubt might just be trying to shield us from the mind-boggling changes that could shatter our cozy comfort zone. We're about to break free and unleash our true potential.

We're all on different paths here, but guess what? We all have a shared destination—a higher vibronic where the illusions, distortions, and deceptions of the world become crystal clear. But, hey, each of us has our own unique way of getting there.

Whether we realize it or not, we're all seekers of truth. It's like a mystical treasure waiting to be uncovered. But here's a mind-blowing revelation: we ARE the way! Forget about searching for external routes to truth. The answers lie within each and every one of us.

And not to totally spoil the end, but it has something to do with you remembering you are love and always were!

Mindfulness: Unleashing Your Inner Sherlock Holmes

I know meditation and shamanic journeying sound pretty cool, but hold your horses, because mindfulness is where the real magic happens. It's like the secret sauce that fuels this entire journey of self-discovery.

When we talk about mindfulness, we're not talking about mindlessly stumbling through life like sleepwalkers. Oh no, my friend. We're talking about cranking up our self-awareness to superhero levels. It's like being the ultimate detective, observing ourselves from the outside and asking those crucial questions like, "What just crossed my mind? And why did I think that? What were the emotions bubbling up right before that thought?"

You see, the trick here is to catch those pesky thoughts that make us feel like we've stepped on a banana peel and figure out where they came from. Think of yourself as an archaeologist, exploring the buried layers of your inner mental and emotional landscape, unearthing hidden fragments and fears with enthusiasm. As each artifact comes to light, it helps to paint a picture of what got buried within us.

And here's the kicker: when we master mindfulness, we gain the power to change our habits. Yep, you heard that right. We become the masters of our own reality, armed with the ability to make conscious choices that bring us closer to the life we've always dreamed of.

Now, let's talk meditation. Oh, there are so many flavors to choose from! But, for me, meditation is like a magic carpet ride that takes us beyond the frequencies we've been conditioned to see and hear. It's all about reconnecting with our most essential self—the expansive consciousness that breathes life into this physical vessel. Here's the catch: we gotta reverse-engineer our way back to that essence, starting with how we feel, both emotionally and physically.

It's time to get grounded and fully embrace the uncomfortable feelings that our subconscious likes to cook up. Trust me, it's worth it. Why? Well, picture this: if deep down we believe we're not good enough, that belief becomes a funky filter through which we interpret everything others say and do. It's like wearing distorted glasses that make the world look wonky. And guess what? We end up projecting those negative emotions onto others, starting a crazy cycle of blame and a never-ending merry-go-round.

We're going on an epic inner adventure, exploring the vast multidimensional wonderland within ourselves. It's like traversing uncharted territories of our own being, uncovering hidden treasures and unlocking our true potential.

Get ready to unravel the mysteries of your thoughts, emotions, and beliefs as we venture deeper into the extraordinary landscapes of your mind. This is just the beginning of a grand adventure that will transform the way you experience reality. Let's go!

Awakening the Heart Chakra: Embracing Self-Awareness, Trust, and Transformation

First things first, we've already established that mindfulness is our trusty sidekick on this heroic quest. But here's the juicy secret: every spirit guide worth their cosmic salt agrees that we have to become aware of the crazy thoughts, emotions, and actions we've been unconsciously choosing. It's time to bring that ninja-level self-awareness into play.

Now, hold onto your chakra hats because we're about to unlock the ultimate power move: the heart chakra! Yep, when we shut down that beautiful energy center, we're basically closing the door to feeling and intuition.

Most of us have been trained to be brainiacs, stuck in our heads like stubborn gum in cosmic hair. No wonder the world has its fair share of problems!

Committing to self-awareness and having the guts to crack open our heart chakra is essential if we want to transcend the unsatisfactory status quo. But, hey, that's just the beginning of the wild ride. We've gotta journey within ourselves, get grounded like a tree with deep roots, find our inner zen, and tap into that inner guidance system of ours. It's like having a GPS that leads straight to the cosmic candy store.

Now, listen closely, my intrepid adventurers, because here's where things get a bit tricky. Listening to our inner guidance is one thing, but trusting it and acting upon it? Well, that's like navigating a maze filled with self-doubt and society's limitations. But fear not, for we have the power to set boundaries with those naysayers and their limited beliefs. Ain't nobody got time for negativity when we're busy manifesting our dreams!

Oh, but the fear…it's sneaky, my friends. It creeps up and whispers, "People will think you're loony tunes!" But let me tell you a secret: those people projecting their fears onto us are just stuck in their own little comfort zones. So let's limit their influence over us and embrace our inner voice.

Here comes the plot twist: we've got to let go who we've been told to be by this fear-based culture. It's time to break free from those fear-based behaviors and embrace honesty with ourselves. Let's be real and say, "Hey, I'm doing this because I'm scared out of my wits!"

Once we shed that fear-based habit, we gain the superpower of choice. We can consciously choose thoughts that make us feel good. It's like rewiring our brain's default program from gloomy to glorious. We become the masters of our own mental universe!

Now, let's talk about the early stages of this mindfulness gig. It's not going to be a walk in the park. We're redirecting massive mental focus toward transforming ourselves from the inside out. But trust me when I say, the results are beyond worth it. We level up our internal set-points for love, joy, happiness, health, and abundance. It's like upgrading to the deluxe version of life!

But here's the beautiful truth: this journey never ends. As someone who's on a mission to remind humanity that love is our birthright, I can tell you that we'll always face new tests and challenges. There will be cliffs that seem impossible to conquer. But guess what? We've got two choices: let fear consume us or take an inspired leap of faith.

Meditation: Multidimensional Marvels

Meditation can be a powerful key to transitioning from a plain ol' mental reality to a multidimensional extravaganza. It's like unlocking a secret portal that takes us beyond the ordinary and into the extraordinary. But before we venture into those higher dimensions, we must take care of our psychic hygiene.

You see, these dimensions aren't some exclusive VIP club where only the chosen few are welcome. They're just different realms of existence, characterized by zippier electron rotations and funky particle spins. And guess what? They're inhabited by some of our most evolved and enlightened aspects.

Right now, most people are stuck in a limited range of frequencies. It's like living in a tiny bubble and occasionally going, "Whoa, something paranormal just happened!" But let me spill a cosmic secret: we all used to have a wider perceptual range as kids. It's just that well-intentioned, albeit fearful, adults told us to zip it and focus on the mundane. How rude!

I witnessed this firsthand during my adventures as a spirit medium. You see, I tapped into my comprehensive awareness and could communicate across a broader frequency range. That's how I could see and hear our loved ones who had crossed over.

When someone transitions back into the nonphysical, there's a vibrational divide. Our dear departed have to lower their vibration to reach us, and we've gotta raise ours to communicate with them. It's like fine-tuning a radio to find the perfect station for broadcasting and receiving messages from the beyond.

So, what does meditation mean to me? It's a gateway to going beyond our intellectual limitations and embarking on a magical journey of emotional and spiritual growth. It's like upgrading from a tricycle to a rocket ship, ready to explore the vast expanse of our own being.

Let me tell you, these explorations are not just for kicks and giggles, although we do have a blast along the way! No, no, there's some seriously cool stuff happening here.

We're talking about an inner technology transfer, my friend. That means we get to upgrade ourselves, our very humanity! Imagine healing in a whole new way, tapping into energies we never thought possible, and making decisions like a boss!

Exploring Further: Keys to Unlocking More of Who We Are

Welcome, my friends, to the ultimate house party—our inner house, that is! Picture this: we're all chilling in the living room, having a grand old time watching TV with our pals. But, suddenly, a few curious souls pipe up and say, "Hold on a sec! Isn't there more to this house than just the living room?"

And so, off we go, venturing into the mystical depths of the basement. It's like a treasure hunt for the hidden gems of our being. We dive into the root chakra, digging up buried trauma, anger, and resentment that we've been sitting on—quite literally! It's time to heal because unlocking the upper rooms of our inner house starts with tending to the basement.

Think of it as a secret code to tap into our magnificent selves. You see, many folks want to skip straight to the upper floors, but the real magic happens when we confront the shadows and embrace the rejected parts of ourselves. It's like remodeling the foundation of our inner house, creating a solid base for our multidimensional adventures.

And how do we embark on these mind-bending journeys? Well, we've got a whole toolkit of shamanic journeying and other meditative modalities at our disposal. They're like trusty flashlights guiding us through the basement of our being, helping us uncover and reclaim those lost fragments of self. It's like an inner renovation.

Now let's talk about the key to unlocking the mind-boggling wonders of multidimensional reality. Picture it as a cosmic set of comprehensive vibrational frequencies where different levels of consciousness reside. We're all multidimensional beings, but we've forgotten. We've been peeking through a tiny keyhole, thinking we've seen it all.

You see, interdimensional phenomena like Bigfoot or the elusive Little People—they've got some serious electron spin skills! They can disappear from our view by changing their spin, leaving us in awe. But guess what? Our trusty pineal gland, the inner eye, has got our back. It's equipped with rods and cone photoreceptor cells, just like our physical eyes, ready to process information from other dimensions. It's time to embrace our inner eye and expand our cosmic vision.

Let's unlock the three golden keys to embracing our multidimensional reality and reclaiming our birthright of love. First up, it's all about taking 100 percent responsibility for our reality. No more blaming the cosmic forces or pointing fingers. It's time to step up and own our free-will choices!

Next, let's turn up the volume on mindfulness and self-awareness. Being conscious of being conscious is like flipping on a superpower switch. It's time to dive into the present moment, catch those sneaky thoughts and feelings, and ask ourselves, "Hey, why am I thinking this? How am I feeling right now?" It's like being the ultimate detective in our own reality show!

Last but not least, we've got to open wide the doors of our heart center. Love, my friends, is the ultimate key to unlock the mysteries of the universe. It's time to let love flow freely, embracing the power of gratitude, compassion, and connection.

Speaking of gratitude, let's make it rain with appreciation. Start your day with a gratitude ritual, listing out everything you're thankful for and celebrating the fact that you have the freedom to choose your thoughts and feelings. It's like a cosmic power-up, transforming you from an unconscious bystander into a conscious creator.

Chapter Two
THE LAW OF VIBRATION

This mind-blowing law states that everything in our universe, whether seen or unseen, is pure energy busting a move in the form of vibrant frequencies. But here's the twist, my friends: it's not just about getting from point A to point B. Life is all about the journey, the twists and turns we make along the way. After all, when our physical body throws in the towel, we all return to the same place of remembering a greater reality. It's like the ultimate after-party of cosmic understanding!

My mission is to help you make some serious quantum leaps in happiness while you're still rocking that human form. We all signed up for this wild ride to see if we could expand into more love while doing the human thing. So, let's crank up that frequency and shake off the struggle and suffering we've mistakenly labeled as "normal."

Imagine you're stuck in a job or relationship that's sucking the joy out of your soul. You decide to ditch the inner complaints and commit to finding something that truly lights your fire. Boom! Once you make that rock-solid commitment, reality starts doing the cha-cha-cha. Life rearranges itself in mind-blowing ways. Get ready for some major life changes as you tap into the law of vibration and take charge of the frequencies of your thoughts and feelings.

But here's the thing: following your heart and making these changes can be tough. You might be going against the grain of your family culture. These folks have their own "set points" for how much joy, money, and whatnot is deemed acceptable. And you know what? We often keep ourselves trapped in this "acceptable" range to avoid the judgmental ire of our loved ones.

Let's renovate ourselves from the inside out. It's like tearing down an old, outdated kitchen to make room for a fabulous new one. Similarly, when we shift to a higher vibration, anything that doesn't jive with our new groove can't survive.

Just like the ever-expanding universe, our higher intention is to expand out of fear and into love. And that's exactly what we do when we tap into the law of vibration. We release old thought patterns, relationships, and jobs that no longer align with our funky frequency. If we keep ourselves stuck in those misaligned constructs, it's like suffocating in a stuffy room. No thanks!

Here's the awesome news, my friends: we hold the key to our freedom. It's called courage! The deconstruction of our old self begins with a deep dive into our identity and sense of self. We've got to become aware of the areas where we're still operating on autopilot, living out some outdated programming.

You see, this conditioning starts early in life, at home and at school, when well-intentioned adults pressure us to fit into their box of what's considered "acceptable." As wide-eyed kids, we try to please people to survive, following in the footsteps of adults who denied their own truth and feelings.

On the other hand, maybe you decided to ditch the whole people-pleaser thing and embrace your rebellious side. Good for you! But hold up, there's a little twist in the plot. Fighting against something still means you're letting that something influence your creations. Sneaky, huh?

Remember that Mother Teresa quote? "I will never attend an anti-war rally; if you have a peace rally, invite me". Wise words. It's all about leading with love instead of fear and anger. That's where the real magic happens.

Guess what? There's a lit new wave sweeping through parenting, education, and even business. Love and conscious awareness are taking center stage, and fear is getting the boot!

So, grab your flower crown, put on your love goggles, and let's join this awesome movement of heart-centered living. It's time to spread love, light, and good vibes wherever we go. Together, we'll create a world that's filled with compassion, understanding, and a whole lot of fun.

Shaking Up the World: Embracing Life's Unexpected Twists

It's time to dive headfirst into the wave of change that's rocking our world. And you know what sparked this seismic shift? The 2020 pandemic. That crazy time when everything got turned upside down and left us all thinking, "What's going on? I thought we were past events like this. I mean, these are modern times".

Just like those personal life events that shake us to the core, this collective moment of deconstruction disrupted the status quo and jolted us from a sense of false security. It forced us to take a hard look at the choices we've been making and the impact they have on our lives. Plus, it made us stare mortality right in the face, a wake-up call that got us reevaluating our priorities.

Suddenly, we realized that we could work from the comfort of our own homes, attend school online, and still be connected to our loved ones. We could savor those precious moments that bring us joy instead of being stuck in some martyrdom program, hoping that someday, somewhere, it would all be worth it.

We also realized with remote work now being an option, we could leave overcrowded cities and head back to nature. But not like the hippies did in the 70s—this time we brought our laptops with us and benefited from all of that serene calm and zen. How do you go back from that? Short answer: you don't.

The pandemic made us realize that we can claim fulfillment and happiness right now. No need to wait for some distant future.

Thanks to this wild ride of a pandemic (and more bumps sure to come), the entire planet experienced a major deconstruction moment. We came face to face with our own mortality and realized that taking life for granted is a big no-no. So, we dared to ask ourselves the ultimate question: "What the heck do I really want to do with my life?"

And guess what? Many of us accepted the invitation to become conscious creators. We said, "Adios!" to those limiting thoughts that kept playing on repeat in our minds, the "I have to" and "I can't" tracks. Instead, we boldly asked ourselves, "Why the heck not?"

It's like breaking free from the shackles of high school schedules, where everything was set in stone, to a whole new world where we call the shots! No more giving away our power and just blindly following the crowd; we're putting on our graduation caps and stepping into a realm of empowered decision-making.

Let's ride these waves of change with style, grace, and maybe a little panache. It's time to rewrite the script, dance to our own beat, and create the life we truly desire.

Embracing the Wild Ride of Freedom

Hey there, fellow adventurers! Let's take a break from reality and dive into the magical realms of video games, movies, and fantasy novels. These fantastical escapes give us a much-needed breather from our own lived experiences and allow us to explore different worlds. But here's the secret: these entertainments actually reveal profound truths about the human experience. We're not just here to survive, folks. We're here to create, and play is our ultimate superpower.

Deep down, in the core of our being, we all crave one thing: freedom. You don't need a fancy scientific study to prove it. Just head over to any school playground during recess and witness the sheer joy and elation as children break free for recess. Those little adventurers run, scream, and leap with unbridled enthusiasm, celebrating their liberation from the confines of four walls. It's a universal language that transcends borders and cultures.

But let me tell you something. Freedom is not just a fleeting moment of recess bliss. It's a metaphysical journey—an awakening to our true essence, our original design, and our birthright. It's a state of expanded consciousness where life becomes less of a struggle and more of a magical voyage of conscious discovery. And here's the kicker: claiming that freedom is an inside job.

We're talking about self-love, self-worth, and self-work, my fellow adventurers. It's about unleashing the power within and embracing our authentic selves. You see, freedom is not something that can be handed to us on a silver platter. We must boldly step up and claim it for ourselves.

Here's a mind-blowing truth: some of the most conventionally successful people out there feel trapped and imprisoned in their own golden cages. They have all the external trappings of success, yet their souls yearn for liberation and deeper purpose.

With self-love as our compass and self-work as our guide, we'll redefine what it means to be truly free. Get ready for the ride of a lifetime, my friends, because freedom awaits those courageous enough to claim it. Let's soar high and show the world what it means to be unapologetically free!

From Stuck to Stardust: Activating the Alchemist Within

Hey there, science enthusiasts! Remember that high school physics class where we learned that energy never dies? It just transforms into different forms. Well, buckle up, because we're about to dive deep into the amazing world of transmutation!

Now, picture this: you're feeling stuck, stagnant, and like you're wearing concrete shoes while trying to navigate through life's ups and downs. It's like being trapped in a never-ending traffic jam on the highway of existence. But fear not, for there's a powerful red flag waving in the breeze, alerting us to the fact that something isn't quite right. We're not where we're meant to be if the flow of life feels more like a slow crawl.

I've got some cosmic good news for you. We can tap into the incredible law of transmutation and propel ourselves back onto the river of life. We're not talking about some casual dip of our toes in the water, my friends. No, we're talking about becoming the river itself!

Here's the secret: when it comes to transmutation, the real magic lies in our ability to take those lower states of consciousness and upcycle them. It's like transforming lead into gold, but on a more metaphysical level. Instead of suppressing or banishing our emotional states entirely, we have the power to alchemize them into something magnificent and life-giving.

We're the master chefs of our own emotional alchemy. So, the next time you're feeling down, frustrated, or overwhelmed, don't throw in the towel just yet. Grab your cosmic spatula and start flipping those emotions around!

But wait, there's more! As we become skilled alchemists, we not only transform our own lives, but we also sprinkle stardust on the world around us. We become the catalysts for positive change, spreading love and light like a cosmic confetti cannon. It's like having a superhero alter ego that uses the power of transmutation for the greater good.

Remember, we're not just observers in this grand cosmic dance. We are the dancers, the choreographers, and the stars of the show. Get ready to transmute those low vibes into high-flying magic and let your inner alchemist shine!

Embracing Your Inner Jedi

Consciousness is like the ultimate power-up in the game of life. It's all about being self-aware, fully owning our decisions, and taking responsibility. No more hiding behind denial, defense mechanisms, or the blame game. It's time to step into the spotlight of our own awareness and embrace our Jedi-like abilities.

Remember that iconic line from Star Wars? "Use the force." Well, my friends, I've got a little secret to share. We don't just use the force; we ARE the force! Cue the mind-blowing music and epic levitation scene!

Just like Obi-Wan Kenobi said, the force surrounds us, penetrates us, and binds the galaxy together. But here's the twist: it's not just some mystical energy out there. It's within us, pulsating through our very beings. We are the cosmic conduits of this extraordinary power.

When we think of force here on good old planet Earth, we often get all caught up in lower physics and push ourselves to meet goals, hoping for success. But, my friends, let me drop some truth bombs on you. You are not just a goal-chasing machine. Oh no, you are a creative force in this wacky, wonderful world.

Picture yourself as a mighty sphere of influence, radiating cosmic brilliance in every direction. You don't have to conform to the reality fields around you. No way! You have the power to project a whole new hologram of reality. It's like being a master illusionist, conjuring up a world that's aligned with your happiest dreams of things like, you know, peace on Earth.

So, let's channel our inner Jedi and tap into the force that flows through us. Feel it pulsing in your veins, sparking up your imagination, and guiding your every move. Embrace your status as a conscious creator, and let your intentions shape the very fabric of the universe.

But remember, with great consciousness comes great responsibility. So wield your power wisely, make choices that light up your soul, and watch as the universe dances to your cosmic beat.

May the force be with you as you embark on this incredible journey of self-discovery and personal transformation. Embrace your inner Jedi and create a reality that's out of this world!

Beyond the Veil: Adventures in Connecting with the Other Side

Picture this: I'm a curious nineteen-year-old, and my parents hit me with the news that my grandpa has passed away. Naturally, my first question is, "Where did he go?" I mean, he couldn't have just vanished into thin air, right? Energy doesn't work like that, and I had a sneaky suspicion that there was more to this whole death thing than meets the eye.

You see, until someone close to us shuffles off this mortal coil, we don't really have to ponder the mysteries of metaphysical reality. It's like we're living in this cozy bubble of blissful ignorance. But the moment our loved ones depart, it's like the universe drops a cosmic truth bomb right on our doorstep, and we can't ignore it anymore.

Now, here's where things get really interesting. I've dabbled in the mystical arts, working as a spirit medium and, let me tell you, our departed loved ones are never too far away. They're like our celestial BFFs, just a thought away from joining us in our earthly shenanigans. They've got this uncanny ability to sense when we're thinking about them. It's like they have a cosmic radar for our thoughts. And you know what? They're not just chilling on some cloud, sipping cosmic cocktails. Oh no! They're actually trying to help us out from the other side. Talk about teamwork!

You've probably heard about near-death experiences, right? When someone's heart stops during surgery and they take a little detour to the great beyond? Well, let me spill some secrets. These brave souls often find themselves floating outside their physical bodies, witnessing everything that's going down in the operating room. Doctors, take note, because these folks come back and give you a play-by-play of what went on. It's like having a spiritual spy cam!

But here's where it gets really trippy. Once they've had their out-of-body experience, they can explore different levels of reality. They're like interdimensional jet-setters, hopping from one vibrational plane to another. They don't need a passport or anything! They just think about a person or a place, and boom! They're there, chilling in the kitchen while their sister whips up dinner or hitching a ride as she drives the kids to school. Talk about travel made easy!

My own cosmic awakening started when my dad got sick and eventually passed away in 2009. I was told by the spirit fairies that he wouldn't be sticking around, so I cleared my schedule and was there by his side when he took his final breath. And let me tell you, it was an awe-inspiring moment. As he made his exit, I was gifted with a high-speed reel of memories featuring highlights of our entire journey together. It was like watching a cosmic blockbuster starring the two of us. Mind-blowing stuff!

And here's the kicker: now, I joke with my dear old dad that he's more accessible to me than ever before. Seriously, he's just a thought away! Forget missed calls or unanswered texts. I can reach out to him anytime, and he's there, ready to chat.

So, if you're longing to reconnect with your loved ones who've crossed over, here's the secret sauce: lead with love. Open your heart, quiet your mind, and raise your vibration. Think thoughts that expand your cosmic field, and watch as the lines of communication start buzzing. It's like having a direct hotline to the other side and, trust me, it's a whole new level of connection.

Chapter Three
TRUST YOUR INTUITION

Life's too short to be living someone else's dream. It's time to break free from the shackles of other people's thinking and unleash the power of your own inner voice. As Steve Jobs wisely said, "Have the courage to follow your heart and intuition. They somehow already know what you truly want to become."

Now, let's dive deep into the mystical realm of intuition. At its core, intuition is like our own personal compass, guiding us toward what feels right or wrong for us. It's all about that sweet alignment.

You see, our intuition communicates through feelings. It's like a divine inner GPS, giving us a resounding "yes" when something is perfectly aligned, a firm "hard no" when it's way off track.

But here's the catch: our cultural conditioning loves to mess with our inner clarity. Picture this: your head might scream "yes" because society says it's the right thing, while your heart whispers "no, this feels so wrong for me." It's a battle between societal expectations and our truest selves. And let me tell you, we've been taught from a young age to be masters of deception when it comes to expressing our true feelings.

Let's get one thing straight: we're not talking about some rigid moral code here. We're talking about what's right or wrong for each of us as unique individuals. It's like a choose-your-own-adventure journey of growth and evolution. What's right for you may be completely different from what's right for your friend on this cosmic rollercoaster of life.

But let's face it: trusting ourselves is no easy feat. We're going against centuries of ingrained beliefs that scream, "You can't do this!" or "You must do that!" It's like trying to paddle upstream in a raging river of societal norms. But, oh, when we finally crack that trust code, it's pure magic!

When we trust ourselves and follow our inner compass, something incredible happens. We unlock a deep sense of fulfillment. We step into a world of vibrant existence, where synchronicities and miracles become our daily companions. We're flowing with the cosmic current, riding the waves of life instead of fighting against them. It's like living in a constant state of cosmic serendipity, my friends.

Here's the kicker, though: society has programmed us to believe that life should be a struggle. We've been brainwashed into thinking that we must toil and sacrifice to prove our worth. Well, folks, I say it's time to flip that script!

No doubt about it making changes in our lives that align with our truth can be scary. And guess what? We often face a tidal wave of negative pressure from the peanut gallery around us. They claim it's concern for our safety but, in reality, they're just projecting their own unresolved fears onto our brave choices.

Let me share a little nugget of wisdom from an Olympic coach. This coach had a gem of advice for his ambitious protégé who was chasing a record-breaking goal. He introduced her to the "rule of thirds."

Here's how it goes: when we're aiming for something huge, something that hasn't yet been embraced by society as achievable, we're going to feel fantastic one-third of the time, okay-ish another third, and downright awful for the final stretch. It's like an emotional rollercoaster.

Why? Because, my friends, when we dare to pursue our wildest dreams and listen to our intuition, we're swimming against the current of cultural norms. We're challenging the status quo, and that's bound to stir up some fear and self-doubt. After all, we don't have the comforting embrace of the collective to assure us that what we're creating is "normal."

But here's the thing: it's crucial to acknowledge the truth. Trusting our intuition can be downright terrifying at times. And you know what? That's perfectly okay. It means we're expanding, growing, and evolving into the magnificent beings we're meant to be. Keep going, my friends, despite the fear, because on the other side lies unimaginable growth and empowerment.

Trusting Your Inner Jedi: Psychic Hygiene and Cosmic Clarity

Alright, let's dive into the nitty-gritty of building trust with ourselves. And, hey, we're going beyond mindfulness here, so buckle up for a mind-bending journey!

Now don't get me wrong. Mindfulness is essential. It's our trusty sidekick, keeping us aware of the thoughts and feelings swirling within. But here's the thing: if we're not paying attention, we become prisoners of our own mental chatter. And trust me, we want to be the masters of our own minds.

But wait, there's more to this trust-building extravaganza! It's time to bust out the chakra system. We're talking about energy centers and their cosmic hygiene. You see, over time, negative energies and pesky encumbrances can accumulate, cluttering up our bio-energetic field like a messy house we've neglected to clean.

So, let's roll up our sleeves and perform some psychic hygiene. We're sweeping out those lingering cobwebs, creating space for greater clarity. It's like giving our cosmic dwelling a well-deserved spring cleaning.

Most of us have been trained to perceive the world on just one frequency level. It's like we're stuck on one channel, missing out on the grand symphony of our multidimensional being. But fear not! We have the power to tap into higher vibrational coordinates, unlocking new realms of intelligence and a treasure trove of information.

Say goodbye to seeking advice from well-meaning friends and family. Bless their hearts, but they're often bound by the same limited assumptions and illusions as we are. It's time to unleash our inner Jedi, tapping into our own multidimensional structure. Within us lies a vast sea of knowledge and wisdom, waiting to be discovered.

When we activate our inner technology, we become the masters of our own cosmic destiny. We transcend the boundaries of what we once believed possible, stepping into a realm where cosmic secrets and profound insights become our faithful companions.

So, my fellow explorers, let's clear out the energetic cobwebs, elevate our vibration, and embrace our multidimensional brilliance. The cosmic stage is set, and it's time to shine as we unlock the infinite wisdom and knowledge that resides within.

Inspiration and the signs and synchronicities that keep us going

Buckle up for a wild ride into the realm of inspiration and the cosmic winks that keep us going. We're breaking free from the chains of overly-rational thinking and diving headfirst into a world where signs and synchronicities reign supreme.

You see, we've become devout students of modern scientific dogma, bowing down to Newtonian physics like it's the Holy Grail. Science has become our new religion, and daring to question the orthodoxy is like poking a beehive with a stick. Trust me, it ain't for the faint of heart.

But let me be real with you. When I first embarked on my awakening journey, I was ticked off. I felt betrayed by the scientific paradigm I had admired for so long. It was like discovering that Santa Claus was just a guy in a red suit. My disillusionment was real.

It hit me like a cosmic slap in the face—the flaw in modern science. Their obsession with objectivity blinded them to the vast array of phenomena and data that didn't fit neatly into their rigid framework. The arrogance and ignorance of it all astounded me.

You see, the problem lies in the limitations of our own consciousness. We're using outdated instruments to navigate a vast universe of possibilities. No wonder we're missing the mark and drawing faulty conclusions.

But fear not, my fellow truth-seekers! I found solace in the tales of history's courageous pioneers who defied the odds and ventured into uncharted territories. From Van Leeuwenhoek, the microscope maestro who faced mockery on his quest for microbiology; to Dr. Elizabeth Blackwell, who defied public scorn to become a trailblazing woman doctor; to Steve Jobs, the "crazy" innovator who revolutionized the world—these mavericks shattered the barriers of convention.

And guess what? Their inspiration didn't come from their puny human egos alone. Oh no, there was something greater at play—a cosmic force that whispered in their ears, guiding them through inspired ideas and mind-boggling synchronicities. Talk about a divine collaboration!

That's why I urge my clients to tap into the magical realm of signs and synchronicities. These cosmic breadcrumbs help us navigate the treacherous minefield of fear that often holds us back. Imagine asking for a specific sign—a red balloon, a cheeky butterfly—and then, boom! it appears, as if by magic.

In the beginning, it feels like you've stumbled upon a secret enchanted realm. But, over time, you start to realize that this cosmic dance is part of your everyday life. It becomes your own personal party trick. And, my friends, here's the key: be specific. Ask for something that can't be brushed off as mere coincidence—a particular number, a vivid color, an object that makes you go, "Whoa!"

Hold on tight, though, because our inner skeptic is a crafty devil. It's wired to deny anything that threatens the comfortable status quo. So, when we're scared out of our wits to chase our dreams, it'll scoff at a thousand signs and dismiss them as mere flukes.

Chapter Four
MEET YOUR INNER SKEPTIC AND CRITIC

Alright, folks, let's have a heart-to-heart about our inner skeptics and critics. You know, those naysayers that hold us back from tapping into our inner guidance and living our best lives. They're like grumpy little gremlins, lurking in the shadows, ready to rain on our parade.

You see, our modern world has done a number on us. We've been conditioned to focus on a narrow band of frequencies, like our old television sets with just a few channels. Anything beyond that limited range was deemed weird or dismissed by the grown-ups in our lives. It's no wonder we've forgotten the expansive multidimensional reality we used to frolic in.

But here's the scoop: when I started channeling spirit guides, I discovered that many of you had already crossed paths with these magnificent beings. Some of you met them in meditation, while others remember them as those whimsical imaginary friends from childhood. But guess what? These spirit guides aren't figments of our imagination—they're real-deal helpers on our journey through physical reality. Talk about having some cosmic backup!

Now let's talk about that other pesky block that's cramping our style—the self-critic. This little devil is born out of low self-worth that we inherited from our ancestors or picked up along the way when people told us we weren't good enough. It's like we've been handed a script that says, "Don't believe in yourself, kid." Well, guess what? It's time to tear up that script and rewrite our story.

We've spent far too long abandoning ourselves. We've handed over our power and authority to external forces, believing that others know better than we do. But let me tell you something: you are the captain of your own ship, the master of your own destiny. It's time to lead yourself with love and courage.

Sure, it's scary to trust ourselves and our intuition. We've been conditioned to follow the herd out of fear. But here's the secret sauce—our greater self has got us. When you tune in to your inner guidance, you tap into a wellspring of wisdom and love that knows what's best for you. It's time to turn up the volume on that inner voice and dance to your own tune.

So, my fellow soul adventurers, let's give that inner skeptic a good ol' pep talk and kick that self-critic to the curb. Embrace your multidimensional awesomeness, reconnect with your spirit guides, and remember that you are the hero of your own story. Trust yourself, my friends, and let your inner rockstar shine bright. It's time to rock this world with love, laughter, and a whole lot of soul.

Busting Through Blocks: Trusting the Truth Within

Picture this: you're in a room full of people, and you hear a whisper in your ear. It's a nugget of wisdom, a message from beyond. You feel it deep in your bones, resonating with truth. But what do you do? You brush it off, thinking, "Nah, that can't be right." Sound familiar?

Well, my friends, let me let you in on a little secret. Many of us are not really blocked—we're just not trusting the information we're receiving. It's like having a direct line to next steps, but hitting the "ignore" button. And let me tell you, I've seen it happen more times than I can count.

I can't even begin to tell you how many times I've witnessed someone receive a channeled message and exclaim, "Oh, I totally knew that!" They had already heard that guidance, deep down inside, but for whatever reason, they chose to push it aside and pretend they were in the dark.

So what's the key to overcoming these sneaky blocks? It all starts with developing mindful awareness, my friends. Imagine yourself as an outside observer, watching the dance of your thoughts and emotions. How do your thoughts shape your feelings? How do they influence your choices?

Here's the deal: if we've been marinating in a sea of negative thoughts and feeling downright rotten, we've got some serious neural rewiring to do. It's like untangling a bunch of messy wires behind the PC—it takes effort and determination. But fear not, for you are the master of your own neural network!

Now let's address the elephant in the room—those deep-rooted blocks that hide in the shadows. These bad boys go beyond the surface level and require some metaphysical assistance. They've become so ingrained in the very fabric of our being that we aren't even conscious of them. They've become our default reality, like an old pair of shoes we've worn for far too long.

But guess what? You have the power to break free from those invisible chains. It starts with acknowledging that there's more to the picture than meets the eye. Open yourself up to the possibility that you can rewrite your story, untangle those deep-seated blocks, and create a new reality—one that aligns with your true essence.

Trust the whispers of wisdom that come your way, for they are the breadcrumbs that lead to your authentic self. It may take time, effort, and a sprinkle of cosmic magic, but you've got this. Break free, my friends, and let your inner light shine brighter than ever before.

Reclaiming Our Center: Nature, Reflection, and Bye-Bye Toxicity

Let's face it. Inner conflict and resistance can be as exhausting as chasing your tail in circles. But fear not, for I have just the remedy to soothe your weary soul. It's simple, refreshing, and oh-so-effective. Drumroll, please...nature to the rescue!

Yes, that's right. Mother Nature is here with open arms, ready to give you the reset you desperately need. So kick off those shoes, put your feet on the ground, and embark on a glorious adventure in the great outdoors. Take a leisurely stroll along a meandering river, embrace the serenity of a tranquil lake, or get lost in the majestic beauty of a lush forest. Ah, can you feel the stress melting away already?

Now here's the secret sauce—leave that pesky smartphone behind or shut it down completely. It's time for a digital detox. Trust me, the world won't end if you're off the grid for a little while. This sacred time in nature is all about recharging your own batteries, not scrolling through your newsfeed or replying to endless messages. Embrace the silence, the whispers of the wind, and the rustling of leaves. Let it all sink in, filling your soul with newfound clarity.

As you meander through nature's wonders, you'll find that your thoughts and emotions have a space to breathe. It's like a symphony of introspection, where you can process your inner noise and begin to neutralize it. Aha moments may strike like lightning, and epiphanies might dance around you like fireflies in the night.

But wait, there's more! If you're in need of an extra dose of re-centering magic, it's time to do some environmental detective work. Take a look around, my dear fellow seekers. Are there toxic people or situations lurking in the shadows? You know, those energy vampires or soul-sucking scenarios that drain your vitality and leave you feeling like you're wearing shoes two sizes too small.

If something no longer resonates with the magnificent being you've become, it's time to bid it farewell. Whether it's a job that feels like a straitjacket, a relationship that resembles a never-ending soap opera, or a community or organization that doesn't align with your true essence, it's time to wave goodbye. You deserve to surround yourself with people, places, and experiences that lift you up and make your heart sing.

Remember, my friends, when something doesn't feel good anymore, it's your cosmic permission slip to make changes. So step into the rhythm of nature, re-center your being, and let your soul flourish like a wildflower in full bloom. You've got this. Embrace the journey of rediscovering your center and watch as the world dances to *your* newfound harmony.

Hushing the Inner Naysayer

Let's dive into the magical art of quieting that notorious party pooper residing within us—the one and only Debbie Downer. Picture her as that snarky neighbor who always rains on your parade. But fear not, for we hold the power to set internal boundaries and shield our confidence from the torrent of negative thoughts.

Now, to hush those pesky voices, we must shake things up and disrupt our neural patterns. It's time to break free from their grip! So get up and skip around the room like nobody's watching. Sing at the top of your lungs, channeling your inner diva or rock star.

Or better yet, step outside for a refreshing walk, letting the breeze blow away those gloomy clouds. And don't forget to take a deep breath—it's a simple but mighty weapon in your arsenal.

Go ahead, take three deep belly breaths. Ah, that's better, right?

In the beginning, those thoughts may race through your mind like wild children on a sugar rush. Fear not, my brave souls, for you have the power to observe them as they zoom by. Give them a nod, acknowledging their existence, and then firmly declare, "Okay, I've heard you, but it's time for a replacement!"

Ah, the art of replacement—it's like a morning ritual for the mind. Set aside precious moments each morning to reflect upon the thoughts that emerge from the depths of your being. Ask yourself, "What's surfacing here? Do I truly desire this as part of my vibrant reality?" It's like tending to the garden of your mental landscape, showering it with the gentle rain of love and compassion. Each thought and fear that sprouts up is an opportunity to decide whether to weed it out or let it take root and flourish.

Imagine setting aside some precious morning time, right after you wake up, to reflect on what's bubbling up in your mind. Ask yourself, "Hey there, thoughts and fears, what's surfacing today? Do I really want to invite you into my reality or should I kindly escort you to the exit?" Treat your mental garden with tender compassion. Weed out those unhelpful thoughts that hinder your growth and decide which ones deserve a cozy spot in your reality.

Remember, you have the power to nurture a blooming garden of positivity and zap those negative thoughts with confidence. Embrace the dance, sing your heart out, and let nature's embrace guide you towards a quieter, more serene state of mind. It's time to take charge and show that inner Debbie Downer who's the boss. Onward, my fellow gardeners of the mind, and may your mental landscape be a flourishing masterpiece of joy and possibility!

The trap of the intellect and the spiritual bypass

Wayne Dyer once said, "The highest form of ignorance is to reject something we don't know anything about." Wise words indeed. If we truly aspire to make the world a better place, we must begin with ourselves. But here's the thing: we need to ditch our rigid intellectual armor and embrace a spirit of openness, curiosity, and humility. Modern science may be impressive, but it's far from having all the answers.

Let's embark on a journey of unlearning and remembrance. I hesitate to call it "learning" because it's not just about acquiring new information. It's about piecing ourselves back together, emerging from the fragmented state we've found ourselves in. You see, I was once a product of that system—acing school, college, and grad school. It gave me a false sense of self-confidence that took some serious deconstructing. Let's be real—the keys to living a truly liberated life can't be found solely within the confines of academia.

Ignorance is no one's best friend, especially when it comes to being arrogantly ignorant. Sadly, there's an epidemic of skepticism out there, where folks hide behind the groundbreaking work of others, arrogantly dismissing ideas without conducting any primary research of their own. It's the classic case of playing it safe while wearing a smug mask.

Now brace yourselves, because when we start sharing our multidimensional experiences, we might just rattle the cages of those heavily invested in the illusion of psychic safety that their limited worldview provides. They'll squirm, they'll recoil, and sometimes they'll even project their fear and anger onto us, fearing that their whole identity is being rocked to its core. It's crucial that we recognize this defensive response for what it truly is—a desperate attempt to protect the fragile fortress of their perceived knowledge.

But hold on a minute. We must also be aware of the other side of the coin. Yes, there are those exploring spirituality and metaphysics who might be a tad too ungrounded for their own good. They get caught up in chasing "special abilities" and knowing "the truth" while conveniently sidestepping their own shadow work—the hard, messy inner work that holds the key to truly making the world a better place.

So let's strike a balance. Let's approach life with a genuine hunger for knowledge, unafraid to explore the realms beyond our current understanding. But let's also stay rooted in the ground of our own being, diligently tending to our shadows and being grateful for their reflection in others. Remember, our personal growth and inner transformation are our most potent contributions to creating a world that's truly worth living in.

We should embrace the thrill of expanding our minds while keeping our feet firmly planted on the path of self-awareness. Together, we'll shatter the chains of intellectual confinement and navigate the realms that lie beyond.

Chapter Five
MINDFULNESS IS THE FOUNDATION

Ah, mindfulness—the cool kid on the self-improvement block. It's everywhere these days, and for good reason! It's like having your very own inner detective who's always on the case, snooping around your thoughts and feelings. But it's for a good cause, so no need to call the thought police just yet.

Picture this: you've got this suave inner observer asking all the right questions like, "Hey, how's it going inside? What thought just made you feel like you stepped on a Lego? Why did you react like a squirrel on caffeine?" It's like having your own personal in-house therapist.

Once you've caught those sneaky thoughts red-handed, it's time for a little editing session. Out with the disempowering ones, in with the empowering ones. It's like being a word wizard, rearranging the magical incantations that shape your reality. Who knew you had such editorial power?

So get your mindfulness game on. Channel your inner detective, edit those thoughts like a linguistic mastermind, and watch your personal power soar. Just remember—be ready for the triggered skeptics and stay grounded amidst the metaphysical explorations.

Practicing Mindfulness: CEO Edition

Alright, folks, let's dive into a real-life drama starring none other than the CEO of a company. Picture this: contracts falling through the cracks, employees slacking off like they're auditioning for a "Laziest Employee of the Year" award, and shareholders breathing down their neck like a pack of hungry wolves. Stress overload, right? So what's our CEO to do?

Well, first things first, they need to do a little self-check. Time to catch those sneaky negative thoughts, like when our CEO mutters, "This always happens." Oh boy, that's a red flag waving in the wind. We often underestimate how much we indulge in these destructive thought patterns.

And here's the kicker: if our CEO isn't careful, they'll end up stuck in a loop, unknowingly projecting those negative vibes that create their own reality. It's like being trapped in a bad rom-com sequel. So, if there's one piece of advice I could give our CEO, it's this: watch out for those self-fulfilling prophecies.

Remember, past experiences don't have to dictate the future. It's time for a mindset makeover! And let me tell you, if leaders can sprinkle this magical mindset dust in their workplace, it's gonna be epic. We're talking about taking that company to the stratosphere. Employee satisfaction and performance will liftoff faster than a rocket fueled by dilithium crystals.

And guess what? This mindfulness revolution doesn't stop at the office door. It's a gateway to unleashing our untapped potential for living in harmony and reaching new heights of functioning. It's like adding an extra sprinkle of magic to our everyday lives.

So, CEOs and aspiring leaders, gather round and embrace the power of mindfulness. Catch those negative thoughts, rewrite the script, and watch your company soar. It's time to trade stress for success and unleash the full potential of your team.

Mindful Parenting: Breaking the Cycle with Love and Laughter

Attention, all parents! It's time to hop aboard the conscious parenting train that's gaining steam. We're waving goodbye to those unconscious old patterns and putting an end to the infamous history repeats itself show.

Picture this: You're faced with a situation where you feel the urge to unleash a yellstorm and channel your inner control freak over your precious little ones. Hold up! It's time to hit the pause button and take a good look in the parenting mirror. Ask yourself, "Why am I so triggered? What's really going on here?"

You see, our children are like little human mirrors, reflecting our own emotions and behaviors back at us. So, if they're throwing a tantrum or acting out, it's a perfect opportunity to delve into self-reflection. It's like a cosmic reminder to reevaluate ourselves and figure out what's going on behind the scenes.

Sometimes, we might need a breather, a momentary escape from the chaos. Step out of the room, take a deep breath, and re-center yourself. Remember, our emotions can easily spiral out of control, and our little ones might just be picking up on that rollercoaster ride.

But fear not, dear mindful parent, for the power of mindfulness is here to save the day! It's time to wave goodbye to fear and violence and usher in a new era of harmony and understanding. Mindfulness allows us to evolve our parenting approach, embracing a more peaceful and compassionate path.

Here's the catch: while using everything as a mirror is key to mindfulness, there's a little twist for our highly sensitive and empathetic parents out there. You have an incredible gift, but beware of taking on other people's emotions as your own. It's like an emotional cloak swap that can leave you feeling a bit confused. Remember to stay grounded and to separate what's yours from what belongs to others.

So, fellow parents, let's embark on this mindful parenting adventure together. Break free from the cycles of the past, sprinkle your parenting journey with love and laughter, and watch as your little ones thrive in an atmosphere of understanding and growth.

Becoming a Curious Detective: Unearthing Hidden Treasures

Ahoy, fellow explorers of mindfulness! Picture this: you and your trusty sidekick, be it your kiddo or your inner child, embark on a daily treasure hunt. But this time, the loot isn't gold coins or sparkling gems—it's the fears, hopes, and beliefs buried within you, ready to reveal themselves.

Every morning, you and your little adventurer ask each other, "What did we wake up with today?" It's like peering into a treasure chest, eager to discover what precious gems of emotions and thoughts lie inside.

Here's a friendly reminder: mindfulness isn't an exam. No grades or perfectionism required. So let's drop the self-judgment and approach this journey with the spirit of a curious explorer, rather than a stressed-out scholar. We're here to uncover the wonders within, not to earn a gold star.

Here's the scoop: our minds have been fed a steady diet of negative, fear-based, and limiting beliefs by our good ol' cultural conditioning programs. It's time to challenge those outdated notions that keep us stuck in a limited mindset.

While it takes commitment and effort to become aware of these belief systems, the good news is that, with practice, they become less powerful. We're rewiring our brains, paving the way for a more positive and expansive outlook.

Here's a tip. Set aside time throughout the day to become that curious witness. Be prepared to be surprised by what you hear yourself thinking. It's like slipping on your detective hat and unlocking valuable information about yourself. Get some clarity on who you truly are, examine the choices you've been making, and decide if they still align with your deepest desires.

Remember, this is *your* adventure. Embrace the excitement of discovery, celebrate the victories, and don't forget to enjoy the journey. With each mindful step, you're one step closer to unearthing the true treasures that reside within.

Oops, I Did It Again! Unveiling Our Sneaky Thoughts

Alright, folks, it's time to play a little game. Grab your trusty timer and set it to chime every hour. Get ready to embark on a thrilling adventure of self-discovery!

When that charming chime goes off, it's your cue to check in with yourself. Pause for a moment and ask, "What was I just thinking? And why on earth was I thinking it?" It's like peering into the depths of your mind and catching those sneaky thoughts red-handed.

Believe me, you'll be surprised by what you uncover. Many of my clients have gasped in horror and exclaimed, "I can't believe I was thinking that thought *again!*" We humans spend so much time lost in the background noise of our minds, unaware of the fears and worries that silently creep in. This delightful timer trick helps us snap out of autopilot.

As my clients dive deeper into this playful practice, they often stumble upon startling realizations. They look back at their lives and recall the echoes of others' words and beliefs. And guess what? The origins of those pesky thoughts aren't too far in the past.

Now, let me confess—I, too, have waded through the sea of fear-based, limiting thoughts. They're like that persistent background white noise, driving us bonkers. But fear not, for a mindfulness practice comes to the rescue, making it easier for us to identify and transform these outdated beliefs.

So, my fellow thought detectives, keep that timer handy, and let the chimes guide you toward a greater understanding of your mind's inner workings. It's time to debunk those limiting thoughts and embark on a journey of liberation. Brace yourselves, for a more empowering mindset awaits!

Chapter Six
THE POSITIVE USE OF FREE WILL

Alright, it's time to unleash the power of free will! You know, that thing we all have but rarely use consciously? Yep, most people are stuck on autopilot, making choices based on outdated programming from their upbringing.

First things first—let's ditch the search for external approval and validation. It's time to ignore the misdirection from others and tap into our inner leader. Ask yourself, "If I were the ruler of my own kingdom and didn't give a hoot about what anyone said, what would I do? And if I listened closely to my heart's desires, where would it lead me?"

Now, let's address the elephant in the room. Why aren't more people flexing their free-will muscles? Well, one reason is that they were never really taught about it. Seriously, when I was growing up, nobody handed me a manual on making my own decisions.

Instead, we're bombarded with well-meaning adults telling us what to think, what to strive for, and what's right and wrong. It's like we're on a track laid down for us, following the same path as our parents. Talk about a lack of originality!

But here's the kicker: it all boils down to our insatiable thirst for validation. We crave the love and approval of our family and friends, so we chase after goals we think will earn us their admiration. We ignore our true desires, and guess what? We end up feeling unfulfilled and wondering what went wrong. Sound familiar?

So how do we break free from this approval-seeking cycle? It starts with cultivating self-awareness. Ask yourself, "Why do I get so defensive about my own thoughts? Who am I defending, and why?" And watch out for those sneaky "I can't" statements. They're like caution signs on the road to conscious creation—they limit us more than we realize.

Now some folks might rebel in the opposite direction as a knee-jerk reaction to their experiences. But here's the twist: even rebellion can become a trap. It's like fighting fire with fire. We need to take a step back and see the bigger picture.

True free will isn't about rebelling just for the sake of it. It's about breaking free from the entire construct and opening up new doorways that lead to unexplored territories. Think of it as an adventure into uncharted realms, where unconditional love and boundless possibilities await.

It's time to embrace your inner renegade and claim your free will with a mischievous grin. Break free from the chains of external validation and create your own path.

Embracing the Overwhelm: Breakdowns and Breakthroughs

Alright, folks, let's address the elephant in the room: overwhelm. It happens to the best of us, and sometimes it even feels like we're on the verge of a full-blown breakdown. But guess what? Breakdowns often pave the way for mind-blowing breakthroughs.

But here's the silver lining: when overwhelm hits us square in the face, it's a sign that we're not on the right path. It's our wake-up call, urging us to question our choices and the beliefs we've held dear.

When we acknowledge the overwhelm, it's time to take a closer look at our lives. Our external reality often mirrors what's going on inside us. So, if we keep finding ourselves in relationships that don't quite work out, it's time to dig deeper. Blaming the other person can only take us so far. It's about time we owned up to our own patterns and choices.

The same goes for any area of our lives that feels less than satisfactory. If something's not clicking, it's time to do some soul-searching. Maybe it's a wake-up call to let go of old fears and limitations that have been holding us back.

Let me share a powerful story. I have a client who went through the heart-wrenching experience of her husband cheating on her. Here's the kicker: she had been repeating to herself, "One day, he's going to cheat on me." Now, I'm not here to blame the victim, but it's a stark reminder of how our thoughts can shape our reality.

You see, our gaps and blind spots have a sneaky way of letting our fears call the shots and manifest in our lives. But here's the good news: we can work on them, transcend them, and break free from the cycle. It starts with being conscious of our patterns and making empowered choices.

For me, these wake-up calls have been the driving force behind making bold, life-altering decisions. Let's embrace the overwhelm as a sign that something needs to shift. Breakdowns are just stepping stones on the path to extraordinary breakthroughs.

From Reactivity to Reflection

Alright, let's talk about self-shaming—the not-so-fun cultural conditioning that's like giving ourselves a good ol' kick in the rear. It's time to put an end to that nonsense.

Here's a little trick that might help. Repeat after me: "Sure, I've got some shame creeping up on me, but you know what? I forgive myself. I wasn't consciously signing up for that shame party. So, let's flush that negative self-talk down and keep on truckin'."

Now let's talk about defensiveness. If something triggers our defensiveness, it's a pretty good indicator that we've hit a nerve—an old negative program that's just dying to take the stage. But hold on a sec! Before we react like a fire-breathing dragon, let's take a deep breath and pinpoint where that reaction is coming from.

You see, the usual unconscious pattern is to go from reaction straight to projection without even pausing in the middle. Someone says or does something, and boom! we hurl our defensiveness all over the place. But here's a nifty little paradox for you: let's de-weaponize ourselves, drop our armor, and open our hearts even wider.

Once we've identified the source of our triggered response, we can consciously decide how to navigate through it. And here's a silver rule: don't take things personally. Picture this—I once had someone turn to me, wide-eyed, and exclaim, "Can you believe what they just said to you?!" And you know what? It didn't trigger a thing in me but, boy, did it rattle their cage. And that, my friends, is how we know it's not about what's being said—it's about how it resonates within us, calling for some serious healing.

So let's kick shame to the curb, ditch the defensiveness, and embrace a world where we don't let other people's words or actions determine our worth. It's time to heal those inner wounds, stand tall, and rock our amazing selves.

Chapter Seven
THE LAW OF ATTRACTION

Most of us are unwittingly caught up in the web of the Law of Attraction, unknowingly using it against ourselves. But fear not! We now have the key to unlock its potential and use it to our advantage. No judgment here—whether we choose to embrace this power or not is entirely up to us. But trust me, my friends, when we harness the Law of Attraction, we unleash a force that can shape a brighter and more fulfilling reality.

Now, picture this: you wake up in the morning, determined to have a fantastic day. You declare it with confidence, only to stub your toe or spill your coffee moments later, sending you into a whirlwind of frustration. Sound familiar? Don't worry, there are two fascinating reasons why this can happen.

First, our conscious intentions may clash with our subconscious beliefs, such as "it's not okay to feel good." It's like having a battle of thoughts within ourselves. To unravel this mystery, we must venture back into the memories of our upbringing, exploring the messages our families imprinted upon us. There, we may discover valuable clues why, despite our best efforts, things don't always go as planned.

Secondly, as we break free from old patterns and transcend our limitations, we encounter the law of opposites. It's a cosmic test of resilience and growth. Just when we're expecting sunshine, a little rain might fall. But fear not, my fellow adventurers, for this is merely an initiation into the realm of conscious creation. Embrace the challenges, ride the waves of opposition, and let them propel you forward.

Many of us proudly wear the "enlightened" badge, but what does it really mean? Sure, you've got the meditation game down, but hey, if a delayed flight can still ruffle your feathers, there's always room for more "lightening up"!

Here's an essential reminder: not every challenging situation is of your making. Your soul's on a mission, weaving pre-birth plans and orchestrating embodied experiences to unlock your greatest growth! So, when life throws you a tough curveball, it's not that you messed up—it's about burning off what doesn't align with love and expanding your heart in remarkable ways.

So, bright lights, it's time to unleash the magic of the Law of Attraction. Let's align our thoughts, feelings, words, and actions with our soul-led desires, and watch as the universe conspires to bring them to life. This chapter is your passport to a reality filled with abundance, joy, and limitless possibilities. Get ready to be the author of your own extraordinary story!

Riding the Rollercoaster: Embrace the Thrills and Stay Committed!

Alright, folks, this is the part where most people throw their hands up and shout, "This doesn't work!" But guess what? We're not like them. We're in this for the long haul. Consider it a thrilling commitment to manifesting our happiest dreams!

Here's a little secret: other people's opinions can be a real buzzkill. That's why I always advise my clients to keep their manifestation journey under wraps. When we're breaking free from fear-based states and transcending into new realms, we're vulnerable. Our reality hasn't solidified yet, and naysayers can rain on our parade. So, let's keep our magical plans hush-hush until we've got some solid proof to show!

But let me tell you something—after a while, with practice and determination, we become living proof of our own power. We can confidently say, "Hey, I've walked the walk. You can project your fears all you want, but I've been there, done that, and I don't believe, I know I can do this!"

As we progress on this epic journey, the tests of faith get bigger and bolder. So, it's time to get comfortable with the discomfort. Yeah, you heard me right. Growth happens when we step out of our cozy little comfort zones and into the unknown. We can't expand and evolve by clinging to our old ways of thinking and doing things. It's time to embrace the risk, the uncertain, and the thrilling, because that's where our soul growth truly happens!

So strap in tight and hold on for dear life, because this rollercoaster ride of manifestation is just getting started. We're here to conquer fears, shatter limitations, and embrace the exhilaration of becoming the creators of our own reality.

Within and Without: Unleashing Your Quantum Superpowers

Picture this: a mind-boggling quantum physics experiment that left scientists scratching their heads in disbelief. Wave particles, those elusive little guys, would only collapse into a single dot when a conscious observer laid eyes on them. Talk about reality taking a wild turn!

Here's the mind-blowing revelation—the act of observation creates reality. Yep, you heard that right. We, as conscious observers, hold the power to shape the world around us simply by the way we perceive it. Reality isn't some fixed, external thing—it's a malleable masterpiece sculpted by our very consciousness.

Now let's bring it back to our own lives. Our perceptions, my friends, can act like funky lenses that warp and distort the shape of reality. It's as if we're playing a vinyl record with a scratch on it. But fear not! I've got the remedy to help you clean out those distortions and repair those scratches.

When I work with my clients, we embark on a mission to remove the errors, omissions, and distortions from their mental programming and energy field. Trust me, once we've tidied up that base code, everything becomes smoother, and people no longer find themselves entangled in the messy webs of polarity traumas.

But hold on, my fellow reality-shapers, we've got some internal work to do. It's high time we showered ourselves with self-love and acknowledged our true worth. We deserve to live spectacular lives and, when we truly believe that, we create a reality that's unobstructed and free from distortion.

Let's tap into our quantum superpowers and create a world where our observations shape a reality filled with love, authenticity, and freedom.

Your Subconscious Superpowers

Alright, my intrepid explorers of the mind, we've got some serious detective work to do. It's time to dig deep and unearth those sneaky limiting beliefs lurking in the shadows of our subconscious. And where better to start than the crack of dawn, when our minds are fresh and full of potential?

You see, folks, it's not enough to simply think good thoughts and call it a day. We've got to roll up our sleeves, dive into the discomfort, and take a peek at what our first thoughts of the day are all about. Don't worry, it's not as scary as it sounds. We're just embarking on a little adventure to uncover the hidden influencers of our reality.

Most of us have been conditioned to have unpleasant thoughts and then swiftly bury them deep down, hoping they'll magically disappear. But here's the truth—true growth comes from getting cozy with discomfort. It's time to lean in, embrace the awkwardness, and unravel the mysteries of our subconscious landscape.

Now, picture this: draw a circle and boldly strike a line through it. Everything above that line represents our conscious mind, where we dwell on a daily basis. But below the line, oh boy, that's where the real magic happens—our subconscious mind, the untapped reservoir of beliefs and programming.

Think of it like an iceberg, floating gracefully in the water. We see the top, but the real substance lies beneath the surface, hidden from plain sight. Our subconscious holds all the stuff we were programmed with—both the good and the not-so-good.

As for me, I've got a fire in my belly to break free from the chains of ancestral limitations. When I look at my daughter, I'm determined to create a new legacy, one filled with positivity and boundless potential. In fact, I was so committed to this fresh start that I legally changed my surname to Love. Yep, you heard that right—I'm breaking free from the past and forging a brand-new one.

Let's dive deep, unearth those hidden beliefs using some pretty cool techniques, and rewrite the script of our subconscious minds. Together, we'll shatter the limitations and dance to the rhythm of a new narrative—one filled with love, possibility, and an unyielding zest for life.

Are you ready to crack the code and unleash your subconscious superpowers? Let's embark on this thrilling journey of self-discovery and create a reality that's truly our own.

Breaking the Belief Code

Let's dive into the wacky and wonderful world of programming. You see, many of our beliefs and behaviors were downloaded into our brilliant minds as we observed the adults around us—those lovably flawed beings who were often unaware of their own unconscious patterns. Our subconscious mind became the ultimate data bank, storing all sorts of beliefs and normalized behaviors.

We have a lesson from the master of comedy himself—Jim Carrey. Picture this: back in second grade, Jim had a substitute teacher who dropped a truth bomb on him. Here's the story as Jim shared it: "I had a substitute teacher from Ireland in the second grade that told my class during morning prayer that when she wants something, anything at all, she prays for it and promises something in return. And she always gets what she wants…As far as I can tell, it's just about letting the universe know what you want and working toward it while letting go of how it comes to pass." So, he put it to the test and, lo and behold, it worked for him, too.

Now, let's take a moment to appreciate this nugget of wisdom. It reminds us that our programming isn't just the result of Mom and Dad's greatest hits. We have an entire symphony of influences shaping our beliefs—some positive, some not so much.

So, how do we shield ourselves from those pesky limiting beliefs that hold us back? Excellent question. Here's the scoop.

Think of it as an opportunity—a chance to take inventory of the company we keep and the media we consume. Yep, all that stuff seeps into our subconscious like a sneaky ninja. So, it's time to become discerning consumers. Whether we're talking about the movies we watch or the tunes we groove to, it all leaves an imprint on our minds.

Now let's get real for a moment. Take a look at the so-called entertainment that floods our screens. It's like swimming in a sea of darkness and violence, with only a glimmer of inspiration and light. But here's the thing: we have a choice. We can choose what we watch as conscious consumers.

Tending Your Mental Garden

Picture this: inside your magnificent brain, there's a network of neural fibers, firing off like fireworks on autopilot. These fibers are responsible for many of the behaviors you exhibit. But fear not! We have a special tool called mindfulness to catch these automatic responses in their tracks.

By catching and acknowledging them, we give them permission to dissolve. Suddenly, those well-trodden neural synapses lose their grip, making way for a brand-new network of trust and faith. And let me tell you, faith here means surrendering resistance and opening up to a more positive path ahead.

So, grab your mental gardening tools and get ready to sculpt your neural landscape. It's time to nurture a garden of trust and transformation.

Once we weed out all those unhelpful thoughts, get ready to witness some mind-blowing results. And trust me, when you see those results, it'll be like a trust fall into a pool of awesomeness.

Let me share a little success story: There was a time when I thought breaking a six-figure income was as mythical as a unicorn riding a rainbow. But guess what? Once I kicked those limiting thoughts to the curb and declared, "No more, I'm going for it!", I freaking did it! It wasn't even that big of a deal, to be honest.

I skyrocketed my company's growth by a jaw-dropping 800 percent in just three years. That, my friends, is a prime example of what happens when we break free from our self-imposed shackles. We gotta look in the mirror and say, "Hey, I've been harboring this limiting belief that's holding me back. But guess what? It's just some crappy programming, and I'm ditching it for something better."

Now let's dive into some quirky scenarios that shape these sneaky neural networks. Imagine someone who trembles at the thought of driving, afraid that any moment could turn into a highway horror show. You know what usually causes that specific fear? Maybe a past-life fender bender or a previous car accident in their younger days. It's like their neural wires got tangled up in trauma.

We're going deep into the past to uncover the root cause instead of just treating the symptoms. And let me tell you, once we start that journey, the clouds of fear tend to clear right out.

We often forget the incredible power we possess to shut off those unwanted thoughts before they gather steam. It's time to set some serious boundaries and tell those negative thoughts, "Not today, my dear. You're not welcome here."

Saying "no" might come easier to some than others, but the key is to find harmony and connect with our bodies. There are now so many techniques to choose from, but it all starts with the will to want to change and a commitment to creating new habits.

Chapter Eight
WHAT'S YOUR STORY?

As we embark on our journey of shredding distortion and embracing higher states of consciousness, let's pause for a moment to explore the captivating world of our stories. We can unwind the tales we tell ourselves, especially if we play the starring role of the victim.

If we truly desire to rewrite our stories and unlock a life brimming with joy and abundance, we must first grasp a fundamental truth: our thoughts and beliefs hold the creative power to shape our very existence.

Here's the deal—it's absolutely crucial for us to understand the stories we incessantly whisper to ourselves about who we are and why we lead the lives we do. Without this self-awareness, our chances of rewriting our narratives become almost impossible.

Here's where things get interesting. Some of you might be tempted to raise your shields and exclaim, "But I'm a victim! Life dealt me a lousy hand!" And you know what? That might be true. Adversity has a knack for barging into our lives uninvited. However, identifying solely as a victim robs us of our power and hinders our growth.

It's like choosing to wear a tattered cloak of disempowerment and then complaining that no one compliments your style.

That's precisely why remarkable individuals who have overcome harrowing experiences often prefer the title of "survivors" instead of "victims." They embody strength and resilience, choosing not to let their past define them. Kudos to these awe-inspiring souls!

Here's the thing—we humans have a sneaky little tendency called self-fulfilling prophecy. It means that, if we believe we're victims, our minds will play a mischievous game, attracting experiences that reinforce this narrative. It's like having a mental magnet for victimhood.

Now let's switch gears for a moment and explore the world of entrenched political belief systems. If someone staunchly opposes a certain policy, they'll instinctively seek out stories that confirm their perspective, conveniently overlooking any positive information that may challenge their stance.

So, what's the point of all this introspection, you ask? Well, it's time to put our detective hats on and unearth those hidden pockets of victim energy within ourselves. We need to become conscious creators, actively reducing disempowering narratives in our daily lives, if we are to claim the happier, more abundant life we claim to want.

Take a moment each day to ask yourself, "What stories am I spinning? What am I focusing on that drains my power instead of amplifying it?" Awareness is the key, my friends.

So when life throws a curveball, instead of uttering the words, "I always have the worst luck," let's summon our inner warrior and say, "Ah, what an intriguing test! How might I respond and find gratitude in this situation? Let's search for the silver lining." Trust me, it's a game-changer!

Questions, Faith, and Winning the Powerball Lottery!

Alright, let's dive into the fascinating world of positive affirmations! We've all heard about the power of affirmation, but guess what? There's a cool new twist to this age-old practice that's got everyone buzzing. Brace yourselves for the rediscovered wonder of positing questions!

Instead of simply saying, "I'm so abundant," folks are jazzing things up by asking themselves, "Why am I always so abundant?" It may seem like a small change, but trust me, it packs a punch. Not only does it shift our perception of ourselves, but it also kicks self-doubt to the curb.

Now hold onto your hats because I've got a story that'll blow your mind. There's an incredible woman I know who set out to win the Powerball lottery. She boldly chose the number $112 million, and guess what? She won that exact amount after four years of focus!

According to her, it all boils down to faith. But what in the world is faith? Well, in my humble opinion, it's like spinning a captivating story within ourselves, whispering it to the universe until it becomes our truth.

When we start asking ourselves questions instead of robotically repeating statements, we break free from the confines of a linear experience. Remember those school days when we were drilled to know all the answers? Well, guess what? We don't have to know it all. By opening ourselves up to the power of questioning, we invite a flood of fresh energy and new information to grace our path over time.

And let's not forget the power of conversation! Have you ever been stuck in a one-sided dialogue where someone just talks at you without asking a single question? It's as exciting as watching paint dry, right? Well, our self-talk shouldn't be any different. Let's make it dynamic, engaging, and filled with curious inquiries!

At a later stage of soul growth, when we've grown into seasoned manifestors, we'll need to surrender everything we've created. Yep, you heard me right. It's like a cosmic spring cleaning, where we release our attachments to make space for future wonders yet to unfold.

As we continue on this magnificent journey, we'll discover that our current creations have the potential to limit our future creations. So, let's loosen our grip on who we were and where we've been, allowing the magic of the unknown to dance into our lives. After all, the best surprises often come when we let go and embrace the grand adventure that awaits us!

Embracing the Void: Letting Go

Alright, let's talk about the infamous void! Yes, I get it—just the mention of the void can send shivers down our spines. We've been conditioned to believe that it's a place we should avoid at all costs. But guess what? When we actually dare to let go and venture into the unknown, amazing things happen!

These mind-expanding techniques we're diving into can work wonders. They help us shed those negative stories and identity constructs we've been carrying around like excess baggage. It's time to break free from those confining little boxes we've been squeezed into for far too long.

Now unless we've got our metaphysical superhero cape on, we might not uncover the root causes of all our issues. However, let me tell you a little secret—we don't always need to know the nitty-gritty details.

As an intuitive practitioner myself, I find it fascinating to uncover the origins of these patterns among the lovely people I work with. It's like finding the missing puzzle piece! But here's the deal: the individual doesn't necessarily need to dig into their family tree and say, "Oh, this limiting belief was passed down my paternal line four generations ago." Nope, not at all.

What really matters is that we identify those negative or limiting beliefs and ask ourselves, "Hey, what am I going do about this?" It's all about taking charge of our own journey. And hey, parents out there, listen up! When it comes to passing down those beliefs to our little munchkins, it's time to hit the pause button and ask ourselves, "Do we really want to gift-wrap this nonsense for our kids?"

Think of these beliefs as family heirlooms. Imagine you've got a collection of gorgeous antiques—priceless treasures, right? But wait, there's also a couple of hideous, grimy artifacts covered in dirt and not worth a single penny. Why on earth would we pass down that junk with the good stuff? It's time to declutter our energy and belief systems and keep only the sparkling gems that truly serve us.

Let's embrace the void and dance in its vastness. It's in those empty spaces that we discover the power to reshape our reality.

Ditching the Uninvited Naysayers

Hold on tight, my curious friends, because I'm about to unleash some truth bombs on how sneaky defeatist entities slink their way into our lives, negatively influencing our self-talk. The biggest culprits include the toxic cocktail of choosing to feel chronically wronged, bitter and angry, as well as ingesting mind-altering substances, like drugs and alcohol. Be careful how angry you let yourself get over well, anything, 'cuz you're risking your spiritual well-being!

My energy-clearing work even showed me that anesthesia can be another sneaky entrance for these entities. Who would've thought, right? When we go under the influence of any of these chemicals, we're basically rolling out the red carpet for these unwelcome guests. But fear not, for I'm here to let you know how to clean up that energy mess.

First off, prevention is key. That means steering clear of mind-altering unhealthy substances. So, say no to overly processed foods, bid farewell to the booze, and ditch the negative media vibes we've already mentioned. Secondly, commit to practicing good psychic hygiene. (More on this in a later chapter!)

When Two Negatives Meet for Tea (Spoiler Alert: No Positives Involved)

Mathematics has its quirks, my friends. They say that two negatives make a positive. But let me tell you, in the wild adventure called life, that rule doesn't quite hold up.

Picture this: you have a negative thought and, oh no, here comes another one. Does that magically transform into a positive one? Absolutely not, my friends. It's like attracting like. Negative vibes hang out with their negative buddies, and positive vibes do their own joyful dance.

Now hold on tight, because we're about to dive into some multidimensional paradoxes. You see, our underlying reality is a product of our individual and collective consciousness. Just as I was tapping away at my keyboard, news broke that a quantum physicist had snagged the Nobel Peace Prize for their work on what Einstein hilariously called "Spooky Entanglement." It's the mind-bending notion that two photons, chilling in completely different places, can be connected in some mind-boggling way that nobody fully comprehends.

Translation: scientists are finally catching on to the fact that reality is a mischievous trickster, playing hide-and-seek with our limited senses. We, as cosmic perceivers, have far more creative influence than we've been led to believe.

Now, let's talk loyalty. As we journey through these cosmic shifts, we might make our family and friends feel like we're rejecting them, their truths, their values, and their carefully constructed identity towers just because we're exploring something different.

Here's the deal: change triggers people. It's a natural part of the process. When folks aren't consciously diving into their own soul growth, witnessing someone else going through that transformative journey can light a fire under their comfortable existence.

Don't let all that negative projection stop you, though. We're all on our own paths and, by shining our light, we might just inspire others to embark on their soul-stirring odysseys.

Unmasking Disempowering Stories

Alright, my friends, let's have some fun and expose those pesky disempowering stories that have been holding us back. You know, the ones that sneak into our minds and whisper, "You can't do that! Who do you think you are?" Well, I'm here to tell you they're just a bunch of imposters, and it's time to give them the boot!

Identifying these sneaky stories is as easy as finding that one thing we keep telling ourselves we can't do. Humans have a funny way of treating those reasons as if they're set in stone, immovable like a stubborn boulder. But guess what? Reality isn't carved in stone; it's as flexible as a yoga instructor!

Here's a nifty trick: when we notice resistance bubbling up in a particular area of our lives—maybe it's our marriage or career—lean into it. That resistance is like a neon sign pointing us toward something significant. It's like a cosmic invitation to dive deep and unravel the mysteries hidden within.

Neuroscience has shown us that our thoughts and feelings weave intricate little filaments in our brains. When those neurons start firing, different parts of our brain light up like a Times Square billboard on New Year's Eve

Many thoughts have been ingrained in us since we were knee-high to a grasshopper. They're wired into our brains like superhighways, zipping along without any conscious effort. Now, if those neural highways are filled with sunshine and rainbows, great! They'll do the heavy lifting, keeping us positive and empowered. But if they're clogged with negative thoughts, well, we've got some reconstruction work to do.

Instead of muttering, "I'm so unlucky," let's bring out the positive vibes and declare, "Hot darn, I've got the best luck in the universe!" Trust me, many of these flips are a piece of cake. All we need is a little twist of perspective to turn a negative thought into a positive powerhouse. It just takes practice. If you catch yourself doomsday worrying about the future, remember to yell "Cut!" and do a retake to focus on what you're grateful for that's going well right now!

We have permission to fake it till we make it. Yep, you heard me right. But hold up, it's not about just going through the motions. We gotta infuse it with genuine belief and effort. Think back to a time when you truly felt lucky, in love with life, and grateful, then embrace that feeling, and let it guide your positive transformation. We don't need to conjure it out of thin air—we're tapping into our very own well of truth.

I've witnessed countless souls who reached this point of epiphany where, deep down, they know the power of their positive thoughts. It's a magical moment, but let's be real—it takes work. We have to peel off layers of conditioning and face the naysayers who try to dampen our spirits. We are the masters of our own narrative, and we're crafting a tale of empowerment and joy.

So, let's rock those positive thoughts, flip those disempowering stories like a pancake, and embrace the journey of reclaiming our truth. With a little humor, a dash of courage, and a whole lot of love, we'll rewrite the script of our lives.

Breaking Free from the Drama Triangle Dance

It's time to dive into the wild world of the victim-victimizer-rescuer triangle. Buckle up, because we're about to unravel the tangled web of stories—ours and others'—that keep us trapped in this dramatic dance.

First things first—let's do some soul-searching. Have we unwittingly slipped into the role of the rescuer? Are we constantly swooping in, cape fluttering, to save the day for someone else? Well, hold your horses, superhero, because it's crucial to ask ourselves, "Is it really my place to play the rescuer?"

While we're busy trying to save everyone else, we need to make sure we're not taking on their emotions. Many folks I've worked with found themselves cast as the rescuer by their families. Why? Well, because they tend to be older souls. Naturally, they possess a powerful dose of self-awareness and open-heartedness, making them prime candidates for rescuing duties within any group they find themselves in.

But here's the plot twist: our aim should be to empower others, not enable their dependency on our evolved presence. We're here to show a different way of being, not to do their personal work for them.

We have the power to break free from this tangled mess. It's time to reclaim our self-sovereignty and make decisions based on our own truth, not the preferences or influences of others. Remember, we're the captains of our own ships, navigating the seas of life with our own compass.

So, let's shake off those entangled energies, cut the strings of drama, and step into our full self-sovereignty. We're here to thrive, not just survive, and by releasing ourselves from the clutches of the victim-victimizer-rescuer triangle, we pave the way for authentic empowerment and a life lived on our own terms.

Thriving as an Empath in a Crazy World

Let's talk about psychic hygiene and the art of keeping your empathic powers in check. We've got a natural tendency to want to help people and feel their emotions, but here's the deal: we need to prioritize our own well-being too. Think of it as scrubbing away the gunk from your energetic chakras on a daily basis.

Let's get real for a moment. Are we deriving our self-worth solely from being everyone's go-to superhero? Are we constantly doing things for others instead of empowering them to do things for themselves? Here's the secret sauce, my empathic friends: doing everything for others isn't actually empowering—it just keeps those negative loops spinning. It's time to shift gears and encourage others to step up and take charge of their own lives. We're not here to play the eternal savior. It's time to break free from those old patterns and let others find their inner strength.

And, oh boy, let's not forget about those drama magnets who have zero intentions of changing. They can suck us into their vortex of never-ending chaos if we're not careful. I've seen it happen too many times—empaths getting caught in the sticky tar pit of their family's drama. But guess what? We can rise above it. How, you ask? Boundaries, my friends. Strong, loving, yet firm and unapologetic boundaries. By setting clear limits, we can transcend the conflict and break those old cycles of dysfunction. Trust me, it's a game-changer.

Now, let's address the elephant in the room. This journey can feel like trudging through quicksand at times, and we might wonder if we're cut out for it. I'll let you in on a little secret: many people fall off the wagon and decide to backslide into their old ways because it's freaking exhausting. But here's the thing—perseverance is the name of the game. Keep pushing forward, my fellow empaths. You've got this!

I've got another gem of wisdom for you. When you're making a quantum leap in your lifestyle, repeat after me: there's no Plan

B. This is it, baby! There's no going back to the way things were because, well, there's no back to go to. You've outgrown that old shoe, my friend. And trust me, trying to squeeze your foot into it now would feel like trying to stuff yourself into your eighth-grade jeans. Not a pleasant experience, am I right? Embrace the growth, embrace the unknown, and never look back.

So, my empathic warriors, remember to scrub away the energetic gunk, empower others to find their own strength, set those badass boundaries, and march forward with unwavering perseverance. You're here to shine your light in a world that desperately needs it. And let me ask you this: Would you trade all the wisdom and growth you've gained for a return ticket to eighth grade? Yeah, I didn't think so.

Embracing the Shadows

Ah, the shadow—the sneaky dimension of ourselves that loves to play hide-and-seek. We've all got them, and they're called shadow aspects. Now don't worry, we're not talking about some eerie paranormal phenomenon. This term "shadow" was coined by Carl Jung, and it refers to those parts of us that have been suppressed or tucked away by our wounded psyches. Our shadows are like mischievous characters lurking just outside the boundaries of our conscious perception.

Why do we hide these shadow aspects, you ask? Well, sometimes we're not too fond of them. Maybe our parents or society judged them, so we decided they're not an acceptable part of who we are. Take boys and sports, for example. They're often told not to be weak, but here's the thing—there are moments when we need to embrace our vulnerability and allow ourselves to heal. It's like flexing those emotional muscles and giving ourselves permission to be human.

Our culture loves to suppress these shadows because vulnerability and weakness are often deemed unacceptable. And, let me tell you, that repression causes some serious damage. It seeps out in strange and unexpected ways, like a pot boiling over with suppressed emotions. Look around—every day, all around the planet, we witness the fallout of this collective shadow dance.

For those who find their way to me, there's a unique set of shadow aspects. They feel unseen, like their intuitive abilities will scare the living daylights out of their family members. They whisper, "I'm not allowed to be intuitive. I'm not allowed to see things that other people don't see. I'm not allowed to embrace my gifts because they scare people." Well, guess what? It's time to break free from that invisible cage and let your intuitive superpowers shine.

Embrace those aspects that have been hiding in the corners of your psyche. Dance with them, learn from them, and integrate them into the vibrant tapestry of your being. We're here to celebrate the full spectrum of who we are, shadows and all.

Unleashing Your Inner Shadow Whisperer

So, how do we become besties with our shadow? First things first—let's shine a light on those shame-ridden corners of our being. Yup, that's the perfect place to start. We need to find a way to comfortably snuggle up next to our shadows. Think of it as inviting them to a cozy fireside chat.

Finding a therapist or a trusted friend who's a seasoned shadow explorer can work wonders. We want someone who can hold space for us without judgment or resistance. Trust me, it's like having a shadow-savvy tour guide.

Picture this: you catch yourself saying, "I really didn't want to talk about this but, hey, let's do it anyway." Bingo! That's a pivotal moment, my friend. It means we're finally tackling those things we've been sitting on, which are influencing us whether we admit it or not.

But wait, what if we don't have a shadow whisperer in our life? Fear not! We can manifest one. In the meantime, let's focus on our inner dialogue. Take a seat, have a heart-to-heart with yourself, and declare, "I know there's a hidden gift here, and I'm ready to unwrap it."

Remember, we need to approach this journey with a gentle touch. No harsh self-judgment allowed! Think of it like encountering a wild animal. When we're in fight-or-flight mode, our reptilian brain takes the wheel, and things can get messy. So, let's handle ourselves with care.

Now here's the real deal: it can get a bit uncomfortable when we start realizing how we've projected our wounds onto the world. Ouch! Seeing the reflection of the harm we've caused isn't exactly a walk in the park. No wonder some folks want to avoid this part of the journey—it's like diving into a pool of unpleasantness.

Let's choose to face it head-on with open minds and hearts. Repeat after me: "I'm willing to explore the unconscious ways I've acted from my wounded shadow aspects. I may have caused hurt, but I didn't mean to. I'm ready to clean up my mess and prevent it from happening again."

Now that's what I call shadow accountability!

Chapter Nine
THE IMPORTANCE OF PSYCHIC HYGIENE

It's time to dive into the exciting world of psychic hygiene. It's all about being self-aware and making sure our energy contributions to the world are top-notch. Let's clean up our act, shall we?

Think of it as being an astral environmentalist. Just like we don't toss litter out the window (because that's a big no-no), we shouldn't be tossing negative, judgmental thoughts into the collective energy field either. We don't want to be those astral polluters, now do we? So, let's take a moment to reflect and ask ourselves, "Am I being a responsible contributor to the collective field?"

Psychic hygiene involves working with our energy centers, clearing out the gunk and stagnant energy thought forms. The results are worth the effort! Picture this: feeling lighter, happier, less burdened and, hey, even less fatigued. It's like a breath of fresh air! Plus, with all that inner clarity, decision-making becomes a breeze. No more limbo dances. You'll know when to say a resounding "yes" or a firm "no" to life's choices.

This isn't just about being a positive contributor to the collective space (although that's pretty awesome). It's about feeling amazing within ourselves and mastering the art of co-creating our reality. And, let's face it, this can be a real challenge if our energy centers are all blocked and weighed down. No wonder so many folks struggle with this stuff. It's like trying to walk through mud!

So, let's unleash our inner energy maestros, clear out the energetic cobwebs, and shine brighter than ever. It's time to be responsible contributors to the cosmic dance floor and create a reality that aligns with our inner guidance. Trust me, life is so much more fabulous when we're sparkling with radiant energy.

To help you out, I recorded a Daily Grounding and Clearing Meditation. You can pick that up by visiting my website and claiming the "Gift Meditation": www.multidimensionalu.com. People have told me it's changed their lives – how cool is that?

Rockin' Your Psychic Hygiene Routine

Maintaining your psychic hygiene is a commitment, a lifestyle choice. Now, when we wake up in the morning, our first instinct is usually to escape from any negative thoughts that arise. But hold up! We need to resist that urge and take a closer look at what's going on inside us. It's time to channel our inner Sherlock Holmes and investigate our thoughts and feelings. Start by finding a state of neutrality, like a zen master chillin' on a mountaintop, and spend at least fifteen minutes reflecting on your inner landscape. It's like a cosmic check-in with yourself and, boy, is it worth it.

Let's face it, folks. Most of us don't wake up with a spoonful of sugar and birds twittering around our heads and singing like Mary Poppins. The density of this planet and the astral field can be a real buzzkill. But fear not! Practicing psychic hygiene is here to save the day. It's a top priority, just like brushing our teeth. So let's make it a non-negotiable part of our routine, okay?

Keeping Yourself Sparkling All Day Long

Let's keep our field shining bright throughout the day. It's all about discernment and knowing when to say, "Hey, that's not my baggage!"

Picture this: Your coworker, let's call him Kevin, is having a major meltdown because he feels betrayed. The office drama is getting hotter than a jalapeño pepper, but guess what? You don't need to jump into that fiery pit of chaos. You can be a sympathetic ear without taking on Kevin's emotional rollercoaster ride. No need to wake up the next morning and realize, "Oops, I've got a Kevin hangover!" Leave that bag of rocks where it belongs and strut away like the psychic rockstar you are. It's all about using that free will choice.

Here's a nifty tool. At the start of your day, set your psychic hygiene timer to go off every couple of hours and then take the time to spend some quality time with yourself. Check in, see what's going on in your energetic realm, and decide if you need a little sprucing up.

Now, let's talk family dynamics. When it comes to psychic hygiene in the family, everyone needs to pull their weight. We're not here to throw our emotional trash at each other like a cosmic game of hot potato. Nope! We're creating a harmonious space where everyone can shine their brightest. Think of it like this: you wouldn't track muddy footprints all over your pristine home, right? So, why would you bring emotional mud into your shared space? Let's keep it clean, people!

To make it happen, we need to normalize open communication. It's all about saying, "Hey, folks, I brought some funky anger energy from work. I'm going to step outside and ground myself so you don't have to deal with my mess." Boom! Simple as that. It's like taking a cosmic walk to wipe off the muddy shoes before you come back inside.

So, my radiant peeps, let's rock this psychic hygiene routine like nobody's business. Keep your field sparkling, embrace that discernment, and don't let other people's emotional baggage cramp your style.

Grounding Like a Boss

Alright, my energetic warriors, let's talk about grounding ourselves and getting rid of all that funky energy. We want to tackle each energy center like a pro, using the power of our breath to clear out any gunk. Once you've got the hang of it, you'll be a clearing ninja in no time. The goal is to zap those pesky thoughts and emotions as soon as they dare to enter your field. Bam! Take that, negative vibes!

A little heads-up. When you're new to this whole energy-cleansing gig, you might experience some unexpected side effects. Nausea, dizziness, and even dozing off like a sleepy sloth are all fair game. Don't fret, it's just a sign that you're clearing out some dense stuff. Think of it as a cosmic detox. It might not be the most glamorous experience but, hey, it's totally worth it.

If you find yourself struggling during the meditation, remember my words: "Stick with it, we'll get through it eventually." The initial sensations can vary depending on what you consider "normal." If you're used to feeling tired and rundown, going through these early stages might feel like a physical detox.

The good news? Once you've done the heavy lifting of getting your field clear, it gets a whole lot easier. You'll become a highly attuned detective, spotting agitation, anxiety, irritation, or any other heavyweight emotions that don't belong in your energetic repertoire.

It takes time, attention, and commitment to understand what truly resonates with you. Believe me, I've been there. I used to carry the weight of the world on my energetic shoulders, thinking it was all mine. It wasn't until later that I realized I was playing garbage collector for everyone else's emotional junk. Talk about a major a-ha moment!

Remember, you've got the power to maintain your newfound awesomeness. Stay grounded, stay fabulous, and keep rocking that energy like nobody's business!

Boundaries With the Darkness

Now let's be real—our society has a knack for obsessing over the dark side. It's like we're drawn to it like moths to a flame, forgetting that there's a whole universe of light waiting to be explored. Just take a peek at the entertainment industry. Goth and horror genres are all the rage, making high-schoolers quiver with delight. But hold on a second, folks. Are we really doing justice to their developing nervous systems? I don't think so.

We need a pop culture revolution, my friends—a shift towards embracing the light and spreading the gospel of psychic hygiene to the masses.

You may recall a little gem called *The Matrix*. Ah, yes, that's as close as it gets to scratching the surface of what I'm talking about. But hold on to your red and blue pills, because even that blockbuster hit left us yearning for more. Unplugging from the Matrix doesn't mean we end up in a dreary industrial wasteland. Oh, no, no! It's an invitation to create our own mind-blowing, higher-dimensional reality. Imagine that!

But here's the catch—distortions abound. If you watched *The Matrix* on repeat like a true fan, you might start to think, "Wait, is this what awaits me if I unplug? Yikes! I'd rather stay in the game, thanks." But, my friends, the reality that awaits us beyond the Matrix is far more extraordinary than Keanu Reeves in leather. It's a universe of endless possibilities, where we get to shape our own destinies and bask in the glory of our expanded consciousness.

So, let's break free from the chains of ignorance and step into the dazzling world of psychic hygiene. It's time to flip the script and bring this vital practice into the spotlight. Together, we can create a reality that's not just the stuff of Hollywood dreams, but a living, breathing masterpiece of our own making.

No Sage Required

Alright, folks, let's talk about sage. You know, that magical herb people burn to cleanse a room? Yeah, there's definitely something to it, but here's the deal—I don't want you to become dependent on external tools like sage cleanses. Why rely on a bundle of leaves when you have the power within you?

Sure, sage can work wonders in purifying a space, but here's the real question: what's the point of cleansing a room if you're carrying negativity around in your own noggin everywhere you go?

Here's the scoop, my friends: it all starts with your intention and will. Just like you set boundaries with those pesky neighbors who always borrow your lawnmower and "forget" to return it, you also need boundaries with the spiritual world. Otherwise, you might find yourself dancing to the tune of malicious entities like a puppet on strings. And, trust me, we've all encountered some of those bizarre characters at bars and wondered, "What in the world is going on with that person?"

That's why, when I'm guiding folks through their deep cleaning journey, I tell them to take a break from recreational drugs, alcohol, all dark media content. Give yourself some breathing room, my friends. It's like going on a sugar detox. If you've ever tried it, you know exactly what I'm talking about. You swear off sugar for a while and then, when you have a taste, you're like, "Whoa, this stuff is sweeter than a unicorn's birthday cake!!"

Put down that sage bundle and embrace your own sovereignty. It's time to set intentions, draw boundaries, and rock your own spiritual cleanse without relying on external tools. You've got what it takes, my friend. Let's shine brighter than the sun and leave those dark entities scratching their heads in confusion. Sage? We don't need no stinkin' sage!

Elevate Your Psychic Hygiene

Okay, I get it—enough about psychic hygiene! But I can't stress enough just how important it is to have a routine for keeping your psychic vibes in tip-top shape. Just like you give your body a good scrub and lather up that fabulous hair of yours, it's time to clear out the gunk from your auric fields and energy centers, also known as chakras.

Some folks out there believe that each chakra requires its own fancy-schmancy process but, let me tell you, that's not necessarily the case. In my cosmic adventures, I've come across more modalities than you can shake a wand at. It's mind-boggling, really.

Here's the thing, my friends—it's all about the basic principles. We're tapping into the brilliant light within us and infusing our fields with our own higher dimensional glow. It's like upgrading your light quotient from the inside out and giving those negative energies the boot.

So let's get back to basics. We want to open up and expand each energy center, envisioning them as vibrant fields of light that just keep getting brighter. It's like having a bunch of dull lead balloons that we need to inflate, polish up, and get harmoniously floating together, shifting our electron spin in the process.

Now hold on tight, because here's where the fun begins. As we unlock these bad boys, all sorts of superpowers start to awaken. But, at this level, the main goal is to boost our sense of well-being by cranking up our vibrational frequency. Trust me, it makes a world of difference.

Just the other day, I had a chat with some long-time clients. One of them shared a major breakthrough. She realized that, whenever she shrinks and drops down into the depths of her being, she loses access to her grander awareness. It was a eureka moment!

Throughout our journey together, she's learned the importance of keeping her field expansive and buzzing with high vibes. This is a massive victory for her, considering the old patterns she was exposed to while growing up.

Now here's the real test of our psychic swagger—spending time with family. Oh yes, those family gatherings can stir up some ancient stuff. But fear not, my fellow soul warriors, because we're up for the challenge. It takes practice, building those psychic muscles like a boss, and when the game is on, give it your all.

And, if things don't go as planned, no worries. Breaking through those intense patterns can be tougher than finding a nickel in a haystack. Just take a stroll outside, clear your mind, and come back stronger than ever. Remember, you've got the power within you to elevate your psychic swag and shine brighter than a supernova.

Steering clear of certain objects

Places and objects hold energy, so watch where you roam and what you bring home. If you stumble upon a gem at a garage sale, don't forget to give it an energy cleanse before inviting it into your sacred space.

Listen to those instincts, folks! If you feel any red flags waving, pay attention. Bringing in that old, gunky energy means double the effort to make things right. So, when I pass antique shops and feel their vibes, I'm like, "Nope, not my jam, moving on!" Let other people's energy stay with them, not in my house!

But, hey, if you're not sure about this whole clearing thing, no worries! Bring in the pros—those who make a living cleaning up energies. They'll give you the lowdown on what's what and, if something's beyond redemption, they'll be honest and say, "Let's leave that outta your place."

The Importance of Psychic Hygiene

Here's a juicy example for you. I once moved into a rental loaded with fascinating artifacts from all over the world. Super cool, right? But. hey, not my energy! So I gave those goodies some TLC by wrapping them up in red cloth and tucking them safely in the closet. Respect for the artifacts and their owners, but also respect for my own energy bubble!

We all get this at a common-sense level, don't we? Ever visited someone else's home and thought, "This ain't my vibe"? It can be fun to hang out there but, deep down, you know where your energy truly resides—your own cozy space!

So there you have it, energy enthusiasts! Clear out the funky vibes and create a space that feels like YOU - vibrant, alive, and bursting with positive energy. Let's keep those energy zones full of good juju!

Chapter Ten
SELF-SOVEREIGNTY

Alright, folks, buckle up for some serious self-empowerment! In this chapter, we're diving headfirst into the epic realm of self-sovereignty!

What is self-sovereignty? It's like being the ruler of your own kingdom, making decisions with pure confidence, zero influence from others, and absolutely no fear of their reactions. Oh yeah, we're talking about walking that path with the certainty of a boss!

Remember the tools we've chatted about so far? They're your secret weapon to reach this majestic destination. Self-sovereignty means breaking free from cultural conditioning and letting our hearts lead the way. No self-sovereignty without self-awareness, folks, so keep that mindfulness mojo!

A huge chunk of this magic comes from our psychic hygiene work. It's all about having the freedom to exercise our free will. Ask yourself, "Am I living in the zone of free will or bouncing around like a pinball, reacting to everything life throws my way?"

When we hear "sovereignty," we might think of royal monarchs in grand castles. But hold up, let's bring that authority home! Self-sovereignty means becoming the ruler of your own existence. Boom! Take charge, express yourself, and stay true to your core!

Shaking Up the Status Quo

Who's ready to rock the boat and break free? We're in a showdown between being true to ourselves and sticking to old-school traditions.

Imagine someone waving the "dogma" flag and telling you to sit down and follow the rules. But you, my friend, have a truth within that's shouting, "No more! Not my jam!". It's like a seed ready to burst through its shell to embrace its full potential—breaking out of old shells that no longer serve you.

Life isn't about playing it safe with a cushy job and a tiny security blanket. Nah, we're meant for so much more! Our souls signed up for an epic game of growth and expansion. So let's claim our true sovereignty!

Unleashing your self-sovereignty is like becoming the hero of your own story. It's not just some fancy title—it's an exhilarating journey of self-discovery. And guess what? You get to paint your reality with bold, vibrant strokes, not by following boring instructions.

That's why I penned this book, my fellow rebels! I'm handing you the keys to unlock your unique expression, throwing away the rulebook, and setting your spirit free! So let's tear down those walls, step into our power, and create a reality that's totally ours!

Ditch the Backpack!

Self-sovereignty is not about strapping on a heavy backpack of responsibility. Oh no, it's more like shedding all those false layers and letting the real YOU shine through!

Get ready for some serious brainpower upgrade! When we tap into our true selves, a whole new world of intelligence opens up. And let me tell you, handling life becomes a breeze! No more hard, heavy lifting needed when you're flowing like a magical river.

When I say listen to your inner authority, forget about the typical authority stuff, where people rank themselves over others. That's not what we're after! It's more like recognizing that we're all part of the same cosmic dance—unique fractals of the One Source, here to enjoy creating and expressing ourselves.

So why hold back? Embrace your individuality and dare to be YOU, unapologetically! You only get to be this version of yourself once—so make it count!

Finding Your Inner Harmony: Being at One with Yourself

How can you tell if you've hit that sweet spot of sovereignty? Well, you won't be doubting every decision like a lost wizard. Nope, you'll be taking aligned action and letting the magic unfold!

Patience is your new superpower. No more trying to control everything like a wild spell gone wrong. Trusting the timeline and trusting yourself is the key. So let that inner skeptic and critic take a nap and enjoy the quiet and peaceful space within, even when the world outside goes bonkers!

Picture this: instead of going all guns blazing 90 percent of the time, you'll find a sweet balance with some quality downtime. And, hey, downtime doesn't mean you're lazing around like a sleepy dragon. Nah, you're processing emotions, healing shadows, and rebuilding your foundation with love, not fear.

No more escapism through overworking! You're here to make the world a better place, and that starts with harmonizing your inner frequency. The field around you feels your good vibes and stabilizes, like a magical beacon of awesomeness!

Breaking Free from Programmed Will: Turn Off Autopilot Mode

Picture this: self-sovereignty is like soaring on the wings of freedom, no longer bound by other people's expectations and obligations. It's a delightful state of clarity, where we connect with our higher guidance and navigate life like magical wizards.

But hold on—programmed will is the sneaky villain in this tale. It's the autopilot mode that denies what our heart truly desires. Like a pesky goblin, it prompts us to suppress our deepest desires and dreams. It becomes so normal that we forget it's even there, lurking in the shadows of our subconscious.

But fear not, fellow adventurers! We've got mindfulness magic up our sleeves to surface all that buried treasure! Our heart, the epicenter of our soul plan and blueprint, holds all the secrets. Sometimes, we may feel lost in the maze, but trust me—we know deep down what we really want for our lives. It's time to unlock that trust and unleash our heart's wisdom!

Oh, and here's a tip: listen to your heart, not your aunt's neighbor's cousin's advice! They might mean well, but their journey is not yours.

When we reach self-sovereignty, the world transforms. We let things flow, trusting our heart to lead the way. No more pushing and forcing things—it all becomes a joyful dance with the universe.

You know what's not cool? The hustle culture that says life has to be a constant struggle, and we're only valuable if we're exhausted and sacrificing ourselves. That's some serious nonsense we need to banish!

Let's break free from this hustle madness and embrace a world where we cherish ourselves, find ease in life, and prioritize well-being over burnout. Who needs illness to give us permission to rest? Sheesh.

Navigating the Advice Circus – Choose Your Guides Wisely!

Alright, fellow adventurers, let's talk advice! When someone dishes out their two cents, do a little reality check. Take a peek at their happiness, joy, relationships, and success. If they're rockin' a perfect ten, their advice might be worth a listen. But, if not, it's totally cool to say, "Thanks, but no thanks!"

Remember, folks, other people's inputs are only as good as the life they're living. If they're drowning in fear and distortion, struggling to find harmony, they might not be the best advisors for us.

We don't have to crush their feelings, but let's not sacrifice ourselves for the sake of being nice. Start by checking their motivator for wanting to weigh in—fear or love? Much of the time, it's fear sneaking around.

But, wait, there's more! Their advice might be based on their own experiences, which may not match our journey. They could be projecting their stuff onto us like a magic show gone wrong.

You know who we often turn to for advice? Spouses and parents—the mighty influencers in our lives. But here's the thing—we gotta unpack their advice and assumptions. Ancestral conditioning, cultural norms, and gender expectations may be hiding in there. Ask yourself, "Are their lives really awesome by my standards?"

So, be bold and let your truth shine! You can say, "Thanks for caring and worrying, but I'm gonna follow my heart and stay true to myself."

Remember, true harmony comes from embracing your authenticity. It's different for everyone, like a whimsical rainbow of individuality. So, face those fears of rejection and failure, and boldly step forward, no matter what Uncle Jim says!

Higher Guidance – Unlocking the Multidimensional Magic!

Alright, fellow seekers, get ready for some mind-blowing stuff! We're diving into the world of higher guidance, a multidimensional state of awareness. Now, I won't bore you with all the complex physics—just know that there's been some disharmony on this planet for a while.

But fear not, for the power to rebuild lies within us! It's time for some serious reconstruction—piecing ourselves back together from within. When we do that, oh boy, get ready to unleash other aspects of our multidimensional self!

One of my clients had a total "Aha" moment—it's not some grand "taada" event, but a subtle awakening. You'll just "know that you know" without a shred of doubt. It's like gaining superhero strength and internal solidity—the kind that makes you go, "I've got this!"

Oh, and get this—when you have questions, it's like chatting with your wise, all-knowing self. Even your spirit guides are part of the cosmic symphony of the greater you.

As a multidimensional being, your greater self is seriously smart. It's a genius at coordinating and aligning things for you. So why not trust this magnificent intelligence on your evolutionary journey? Let it guide you toward the grandest version of yourself!

It's time to believe in YOU, my friend. No need to rely on some external guru—you've got the purest, most magical version of yourself to turn to.

Reclaiming Our True Selves

Sovereignty is like a superhero power, giving us the ability to be the conscious actors and creators of our own lives. We refuse to hand over our power to anyone and, if it slips away, we quickly recognize it and reclaim it.

Our sovereignty and conscious creation are a magical duo, each boosting the other. It's a dynamic process, propelling our soul's evolution forward. As we act upon our truths, trust them, and let them grow, we become the architects of our reality.

Here's the secret sauce—when we reach this state, negativity can't mess with us anymore. We'll be in a self-sustaining zone, confidently saying "no" to any negativity that comes our way. How cool is that?

But, wait, there's more! We might need to bid farewell to our former selves—our lower ego self, to be precise. Shamans call it "the little death" and, yeah, it can bring some real grief. It's like saying goodbye to old identity constructs and the familiar comfort zone.

I'll never forget my own little "goodbye" moment. My former self asked, "Are you sure you don't need me?" But I firmly replied, "I'm sure, thank you for everything!" And off it went into the sunset. From time to time, it sneaks back, but I just reassure it to enjoy the ride and chill in the back seat.

Surrendering the old identity can feel scary—it's uncomfortable at first. We've derived a sense of safety and security from it. But, trust me, our soul yearns to grow beyond that limited space.

No judgments here, though—we're free to decide our path. Personally, I believe embracing the growing pains leads to big leaps and self-liberation. Not fun in the moment but, dang! how did I get so tall?

So let's take the journey of reclaiming our true selves, embracing sovereignty, and writing a fantastic adventure of growth, love, and magic!

Embracing Empowered Choices

First things first—no judgments here! If we've given our power away in the past, it's all part of the valuable experience that shapes our journey.

In the early stages of life, our family programming often sets the stage, providing us with some valuable contrast for what truly resonates with us.

All these experiences contribute to where we are today. Instead of resenting our programming, let's practice gratitude for the valuable contrast it offered. It's like saying, "Thanks for the lessons, but it's time to step into my authentic self and make decisions from a place of deep knowing. I have clarity because I know what I don't want."

Just like we can't have light without darkness, knowing what we don't want helps us navigate life's choices. We don't need to prove anything to anyone. We can let out our ego, accustomed to seeking approval and validation, take a rest. Instead, we embrace the perspective that everything just is—no need for those "right or wrong" games.

A universal truth emerges. We all fear being wrong, but guess what? What's wrong for one may be right for another. Reality turns out to be more subjective than we think.

So, let's step into our empowered choices, embrace the beauty of contrast, and journey through life with the wisdom of our authentic selves!

Rising from Faulty Foundations

Hey, don't beat yourself up! It's not about wasting the first half of life—it's about gaining clarity on where we've been, where we are, and where we want to be. It's time for some soul renovation—keep what serves you and leave the rest behind.

Loads of folks are waking up and realizing that their work and relationships don't fit anymore. They're like, "Whoa, the foundation of my marriage was built on distortion, and it's time to let go. But, hey, at least now I understand why I bought into it."

No need to feel ashamed about those faulty foundations—it's something we inherited. We all face sticky emotions as we go through this process. Society likes to make us feel bad about getting things wrong, but that's just cultural mumbo-jumbo.

My mission is to help you dissolve that shame, open your heart chakra, and embrace self-love. It's the ultimate cure for everything that ails humanity. So let's rise above those shaky foundations and build a brighter future!

Rising Above "Us and Them"

Stepping into our self-sovereignty means ditching the old "us and them" mindset. No more getting manipulated into polarized thinking or getting sucked into drama and victim stories. We rise above taking sides and gossiping. It's time for a neutral perspective where we see all sides of the story.

The "us and them" mentality is like splitting ourselves in two—it's divisive and feels downright slimy. Sure, it's a valid experience, but we don't want to get stuck in that muck.

During our awakening journey, we might uncover some ugly truths about power abuses and the state of the world, and it's natural to feel angry. But we mustn't linger there, or we'll drain our power and perpetuate more conflict.

This divisive mentality is rampant in our society, especially online, where divisive content gets more clicks and more profit for social media platforms. But, as self-sovereign beings, we can see through the clickbait and stay grounded in love.

Self-sovereignty also means recognizing that everyone is a part of the Source. So we treat others with respect, kindness, and compassion while maintaining healthy boundaries. We're not doormats; we're empowered individuals creating a better world!

The Power of Zero Point

There's a magical place called the zero point, where we can maintain a neutral position even in the face of human reactions to injustice. In this state, we avoid becoming puppets controlled by anger, and we retain full possession of our senses.

The zero point is where our true power lies. By aligning our energy field with this neutral state, we gain the ability to navigate and stabilize the collective drama that surrounds us.

Remaining neutral allows us to tap into oneness, where solutions based on cooperation and harmony can emerge. It's a shift from the divisive "us and them" mentality to a unified "we" mentality. From this place of unity, winning solutions that benefit everyone can arise.

Chapter Eleven
SETTING HEALTHY BOUNDARIES

Alright, it's time to unleash your inner Boundary Ninja and rock those healthy boundaries like a boss! If you've struggled with people-pleasing, fear not, we've got your back with some cool tips and tricks to honor your truth.

Picture this: you, clad in your ninja gear, gracefully saying "no" to anything that doesn't serve your soul's purpose. No more feeling obligated to do things you don't want to do. Sayonara, people-pleasing!

Remember, there's no universal right or wrong when it comes to personal choice—it's all about what feels right for you. So, let's meet Rumi in that awesome field beyond ideas of wrongdoing and rightdoing. It's a field of pure freedom, my friend!

We're here because we crave a vibrant life, where joy, expansion, and freedom flow like a river. So, let's dive into the art of knowing your true no from your heartfelt yes. It's like mastering the ancient ninja techniques, but for your soul.

It's time to break free from the chains of conformity and embrace your unique self. When faced with those group decisions, ask yourself, "Is this what I truly feel?" Unleash your ninja skills and tap into all those super techniques we've learned together.

Get ready to rock those boundaries and dance to your soul's rhythm. With ninja-like precision, you'll navigate life like never before. So, gear up, my fellow Boundary Ninja, and let's embark on this epic journey of self-discovery together!

Breaking Free: Embracing the Power of Opting out

Picture this: you, the fearless opt-out champion, standing tall amidst the crowd of conformity. You know why you want to opt out, and it's because you crave a better life. It all starts within, my friend, and no amount of activism can fill that void.

Now, here's the secret sauce: saying "yes" when you mean "no" only reinforces the reality you're trying to escape! It's time to break free from that cycle and own your truth.

So, muster up the courage to say "NO" loud and clear. In this defining moment, epiphanies are bursting like fireworks, and people are questioning the norm. Just because it's normal doesn't mean it's healthy or functional, right?

And guess what? Our families can be the ultimate showdown in our awakening journey. They've known us forever, or so they think! If they're not on the growth-oriented bandwagon, they might resist our evolution. But fear not, my brave soul, they're just playing the part they agreed to play in your pre-birth planning session!

The Yes Scale and Liberating Boundaries

Alright, it's decision time! Say hello to the fabulous Yes Scale, your trusty tool for determining the worthiness of saying "yes." Picture this: you're engaging in something, and you rate your excitement on a scale of one to ten. If it's below a sparkling seven, pause and ponder, my friend. Why are you even in this game?

Give yourself the ultimate gift of permission: "Uncle Jim's not my cup of tea. Why am I sipping tea with him?" Liberating, right?

But hold on, the real magic is yet to come! Let go of trying to change those around you. Embrace the power to retreat, spend less time, or even cut off contact if needed. It's your life, and you hold the reins!

Ah, the final frontier: our upper echelons of manifestation. Here, we face the subtle ways we play a part in those old constructs. We might have seen ourselves as passive victims, blaming others for imposing their realities. But, wait, we also seek their approval, which keeps us tangled in the dance.

Ready for the breakthrough? Once we shed the need for their validation, the energy dynamics flip! It's pure empowerment, my friend. I've witnessed it in myself and countless others. We might have been the rescuers, but no more! Liberating others by freeing them from our clutches.

Now let's be real. Establishing boundaries can be one sticky affair. Justifying and deflecting like acrobats! "I can't do that, I have to do this!" Oh, those pesky cultural obligations, they won't let go without a tango.

I've had my fair share of walking away from disharmonic situations that didn't resonate with my soul. And, let me tell you, it's been eye-opening!

Surprisingly, those who chose to stick around and observe have noticed something fascinating. My departure seemed to act as a catalyst for change. It's like my stepping away from the old sparked a ripple effect, nudging the energies towards a different direction.

Sometimes, our bravest choices become a beacon for others, inviting them to seek their own truth and liberation. Change begins with one courageous step!

Tuning in to Your Truth

Get ready to have your mind blown by this totally rad concept I explored with a client: we're like tuning forks, baby! Picture this: whenever we're in a conversation, mulling over ideas, or tackling work stuff, we imagine ourselves as tuning forks and ask, "Is this vibe resonating with my soul? Is it giving me good vibes or dragging me down?" How epic is that for finding our true north?

You won't believe it, but this tuning-fork trick worked like magic for my client! It gave them the cosmic courage to make a bold move—they finally dropped their resignation letter after years of wanting to quit their job. Sure, they had some fears about what comes next—uncertainty, financial stuff, and even the dreaded possibility of couch-surfing. But guess what? They realized those fears were just old echoes, conditioned responses messing with their cosmic groove.

Oh, and here's a cosmic tale that'll have you nodding your head in agreement! So there's this inspiring talk I stumbled upon where a guy was launching several new businesses. But, when they shared their stoked excitement with their dad, he hit 'em with some statistics about new businesses failing. Bummer, right? But, wait for it—they learned the art of setting boundaries! They decided to keep their dreams safe and keep the conversation to surface-level topics with the old man.

Now let's be real. Setting boundaries can be a bit like navigating a cosmic obstacle course, especially with family. But you know what?

Sometimes, we gotta let go of those relationships that mess with our cosmic groove. Not everyone's ready for the cosmic adventure of self-discovery, and that's totally cool. We're all on our own journeys, and that's what makes life a wild and wonderful ride!

So instead of being all judgy and harsh, let's show some cosmic compassion! We can groove to our own beats and be an inspiration for others when they're ready to dance to their own tunes.

Here's the cherry on top: we don't need everyone to walk in our footsteps! By setting boundaries, we can glide more gracefully through life, vibing with peeps who groove on our wavelength. No more stressing about what others think! We can be our authentic selves, embracing the magic of this cosmic journey with pure joy and wonder.

So let's crank up the volume on our inner rockstar and let the universe hear our soulful melodies! Embrace the cosmic adventure, my friends, and remember: you're a rockstar tuning fork, and the universe is your stage!

Navigating Mind Games and Unspoken Expectations

We're bombarded with assumptions and unspoken expectations. It's like living in a world of passive communication, where things are rarely spoken and even more rarely actually communicated.

But hold up, let's be real about making commitments! When we say, "Yes, I'll get this project done on time," it's about giving it our best shot, right? If we miss the mark, well, at least we tried our darn best.

Now check this out: when Aunt May guilt-trips us for not meeting her invisible expectations, but we never had a real talk about it, we don't owe her squat! No matter what she says, it's not our problem.

The real problem is when we start speaking in riddles and innuendos. Someone might say, "If you don't want to hang out, it means you don't love me." But come on, that's just them dealing with their own issues! It's not our job to make people happy, especially if they aren't up for the inner work on their own self-love.

And let's talk about those co-dependent relationships, the ones that sometimes feel like a cosmic whirlwind. It's tricky, right?

But fear not, cosmic adventurers, because we've got the key to self-sovereignty! We're responsible for our own source of love, validation, and approval. As long as we're taking care of ourselves internally, we're on the right track. Any validation from outside is just a little extra cosmic sparkle!

But let's be real: planet Earth has its fair share of co-dependency and twisted relationship patterns. We need to shift to a more balanced and harmonious way of living, based on self-love and self-sovereignty.

So what's self-sovereignty all about? It's saying, "I'm 100 percent responsible for my feelings, all day, every day." Sure, we might slip up and project our mess onto our loved ones, but we gotta clean up our act, y'all!

Now here's the cosmic shift we need: forget the idea that we have to bend over backward to keep everyone happy. Nah, let's participate when it feels right but, remember, everyone's responsible for their own vibes.

Passing On Positive Vibes to the Next Generation

Hey there, awesome parents and anyone who cares about the world's children. Let's talk about raising the next-gen and passing on some serious goodness. With all the challenges in the world, it can be a wild ride to set healthy boundaries and be the best version of ourselves. But, hey, we got this!

I've got this fabulous 17-year-old daughter, and we've been on quite a journey together. Teaching her the art of self-love is my top priority, and I'm not just talking about it, but living it.

You know what's super cool? We have the power to break old patterns that have been passed down from past generations. Our conscious-parenting game is strong, and the world is taking notice with a bunch of great resources and inspiring leaders emerging.

So, raising a conscious child means helping them to recognize their inherent worth, regardless of any accomplishments. It also means teaching them how to watch the inner ticker tape of their mind and how to make some edits! And guess what? We can do it right from the start! No waiting around for them to take on a bunch of negative stuff and then fixing it later.

Sure, when they start school, they'll pick up stuff from others who haven't done this work. But fear not! The incoming kids are a different breed. They're not buying into the same old stuff like we did. So our role is to show them that they're valuable just as they are, no strings attached!

So let's pass on that positive energy to the next generation! We're raising confident and emotionally resilient individuals who know their worth and embrace their feelings. It's time to break free from the old patterns and create a world where everyone shines brightly!

Chapter Twelve
CREATE YOUR FUTURE

By now, you've realized that you might have been unconsciously cooking up some less-than-desirable life experiences. But guess what? With our conscious free will and some stellar psychic hygiene, we can whip up something absolutely amazing! Say goodbye to dysfunction, fear, and worry. We're stepping into a whole new groove!

You know, we could choose to focus all our energy on fear of ending up homeless, or we could flip the switch and focus on being magnets for prosperity and abundance. It's all about where we choose to put our attention—no judgment!

Sure, the human family has normalized rockin' the negative vibes, but we're not letting that hold us back! With some mindful mojo, breath work, and psychic cleanliness, we can rock this cosmic recipe.

So, the first step to creating our future is taking a chill pill and looking at things objectively. We've got this expanded awareness, and now it's time to ask ourselves, "Hey, what do I want to do with this epic free will choice?"

Rethinking the Dumpster Fire and Igniting the Good Vibes

You know what's weird? The media and news love to paint the world as a giant dumpster fire and, when we buy into that, our perception gets all wonky. But guess what? We can change the channel and start projecting a whole new show from within!

Imagine if every single person on this amazing planet did that. Boom! We'd be living in a totally different world!

Here's the cosmic scoop: in our own little galaxy of thoughts and emotions, we have more power than we've been told. Seriously, it's like we're cosmic wizards in our own right! The big idea in this chapter is to take all the cool stuff we've learned so far and cook up some fun new creations!

Let's Make This Thought Game Fun and Super Simple

Alright, let's break this down in the easiest way possible. You know how when we keep thinking about something over and over, it kinda sticks? Well, it's like a prayer in reverse. Not cool, right?

Every single morning, we have a choice. We can re-pattern our thoughts and set our autopilot to expansion and unconditional self-love. Even if a negative thought creeps in, we'll be ready to handle it like a champ!

When we do this magic right, it taps into the law of attraction and manifestation. We get to dive deep into our goals and cosmic vision, using all the rad techniques we've learned in this book. Before we know it, our cosmic reality will be one we absolutely love, and no more "Ugh, here we go again"!

The attitude of gratitude is a total classic. You've heard about it a zillion times, and you know what? It really works! Instead of focusing on what's missing in our lives, let's celebrate what we already have.

When we fill our hearts with gratitude, our vibes shift, and something magical happens! We leave behind the heaviness and embrace a whole new reality. It's like being magicians of positivity, projecting our dreams out into the world!

Our subconscious holds a treasure trove of memories, and that's why these tools and techniques are so essential. They help us clear out the old stuff, so we can respond consciously rather than react blindly.

Responsibility means we get to steer our own cosmic ship, consciously choosing our reactions. It's like being the captain of our lives, making intentional choices every step of the way!

Life is a Canvas of Creation

Every single moment is a chance to paint our own masterpiece! We're the artists of our lives, which means, if we're not digging our current reality, we can totally change it!

Let's focus on the future: today is the foundation for tomorrow's creation! When we shift our present, we're setting a whole new reference point for what's to come.

Imagine someone stuck in a job they're not thrilled about. Here are two approaches: first, we can pretend we're in the dream job while we're still there, using our emotions to manifest the real deal. Cosmic visualization, baby!

Or, option number two: we can take a leap of faith, hand in our notice, and create a void. It's a deconstruction that clears space for something better to emerge. Both paths are totally legit—just do what feels right for you!

What *won't* work? Staying stuck in a job we hate and just complaining to everyone about it! Nope, that's not gonna change anything.

I've taken the cosmic leap of faith myself many times! Plus, I've watched my awesome clients do the same thing. When we set ourselves up for success, the universe has a way of stepping in with amazing "you won't believe what happened" kinda opportunities.

We're constantly creating our reality with the power of our thoughts and feelings. So let's level up our cosmic skills by boosting our self-awareness, bringing those shadows to light, and raising our vibes to a higher frequency!

Check it out: imagine our heart chakra and our mind's eye joining forces like superheroes! They meet at a point, and bam! we become walking movie projectors, creating our very own holographic reality. How cool is that?

Here's the twist: each of us has our own unique movie playing! No two experiences are the same, and that's the beauty of it all.

So let's get conscious and ask ourselves, "What's playing on the screen of my mind? Fearful thoughts or a dazzling future of my dreams?"

Let's Flip the Script: Embrace, Expand, and Create

Here's a universal truth: what we resist persists, like gum on the bottom of our shoe! So let's shake things up and redirect our focus towards what we really want. By setting our sights on the outcomes we desire, we can manifest the reality of our dreams!

Sometimes, though, we hit roadblocks. Our subconscious might be pulling us in the opposite direction, like magnets gone haywire! It's like the conscious mind says, "I want it," but the subconscious says, "Nope, not gonna happen!" That's why re-programming the subconscious, using one of many super-cool modalities now available, is so important.

Let's talk about those big dreams! Sure, some folks want fancy cars and shiny watches but, deep down, we're talking about soul-level desires. Think starting a family, opening a healing retreat center, making inspired movies, or becoming a full-time artist!

When we break free from the illusion of comfort and security, it's an awakening! We realize we can have so much more by living in our most expansive, joyful, on purposeful state.

Here's the secret: we're a limitless wellspring of creativity and resourcefulness, a fractal of the One Source! No more getting stuck in dreary jobs for perks! We've got the power to provide for ourselves, and that well never runs dry!

Embrace Your Unique Path: Trusting the Soul's Plan

We might occasionally feel some doubt but, remember, those desires and dreams in our hearts are part of our soul blueprint. So, believe in the plan we crafted before we even began this journey. Keep the energy flowing and take aligned action!

Here's where the challenge lies—many of us stumble when it's time to make a move. Take my friend, for instance—she had a secure job, but her heart urged her to go back to school to pursue a different role in her company. The only problem? Family commitments and a busy schedule made it daunting!

But here's where the magic happens—her intuition made it crystal-clear that she had a special gift in that field. That's what she was meant to do! Sure, she worried about practicalities, but her instincts reassured her. And you won't believe it—things fell into place, she found success in her new venture, and she now owns the company!

Note: our loved ones might not fully understand our path, and that's okay. Sometimes, we don't even have all the answers ourselves. We just feel the calling deep within!

So, brave souls, let's embrace our unique paths and trust the plan unfolding before us! Our journey might seem mysterious to others, but we're following the compass of our hearts, and that's all we need to move forward with confidence!

Taking Aligned Action: Curating Joy and Embracing the Adventure

Taking aligned action is where the real magic happens, but I get it—it can be a bit nerve-wracking. Suddenly, those private conversations with ourselves are about to meet the big, wide world! And, yes, making big changes might cause some raised eyebrows among family and friends but, hey, it's all part of the adventure!

Sure, breaking free from old constructs and boxes can feel scary, especially when they used to give us a sense of security. But when that box starts suffocating us, it's a clear sign we've outgrown it! Time to spread our wings and soar!

Now here's the secret sauce to success: set some fabulous boundaries and keep those negative influences at bay. When we're sovereign, we're unstoppable, and fear and doubt can't dim our luminescence!

Let's ditch the notion of right and wrong and embrace every experience and exploration. It's all about giving it our best shot and enjoying the journey. Remember, regrets are for things we didn't do, not for the adventures we embarked on!

Create Your Future

Take a cue from Spielberg, the movie maestro himself! He faced a lot of rejection early on, but didn't let it dim his dream. Persistence paid off, and the world got to enjoy his incredible creations!

Now here's a little daily hack for joy: curate joy like it's your personal masterpiece! Swap the news for some soul-lifting happy jazz on YouTube or whatever tickles your fancy. Make it a morning ritual, and watch your spirit soar!

Even during the hustle and bustle of our daily lives, we all still have some free time. Use it wisely! Instead of wallowing in job dissatisfaction, shift your focus and see it as a temporary stop on the adventure. We're shifting ourselves from within, creating in our inner landscape, and eagerly awaiting the next marvelous manifestation!

Guess what? With practice, taking aligned action becomes a piece of cake! Hesitation and second-guessing? Out the window! You'll be standing tall and showing yourself just how incredible you can be!

Chapter Thirteen

WHAT'S YOUR SOUL PURPOSE?

Alright, folks, let's get cozy and dive into the heart of it all: our soul purpose! You see, being here in this human form is like a grand cosmic playground. We're all here for the fun, the experience and, of course, some soul growth. Whether you're a seasoned soul or a newbie, we're all in this together, learning and growing.

Now, picture this: we are all interconnected fractals of the One Source, just like little puzzle pieces making up the big love-filled Universe. It's like playing a game of "hide-and-seek" with ourselves, deliberately forgetting our cosmic connection to have a human experience. And, boy, does that experience come with some twists and turns: density, distortion, fear, worry, judgment, and competition—the works!

But here's the thing—at some point, our souls say, "Hey, let's level up and leave those lower states of consciousness behind!" We've seen the not-so-pleasant side of it all, and we're ready to elevate ourselves back into a higher remembering. That's what drives us to make the changes we've been chatting about in this book.

And guess what? You, my friend, have decided to take that cosmic U-turn for home! You've gathered valuable experiences and wisdom along the way, and now you're all set to move forward in this human journey with a clear sense of soul purpose.

By now, everything we've explored in the previous chapters should be clicking into place. We're challenging old conditioning and societal norms, all because there's a beautiful flame burning inside you, telling you, "Hey, there's something special you're meant to do!" That, my dear, is your soul purpose shining bright.

For all you old souls out there, get ready for the fun part of being human! It's time to ditch the societal expectations and embark on a journey of deep inner referencing and incredible outer alignment. The adventure is just getting started, and it's going to be amazing! So, let's embrace our soul purpose with a big warm hug and keep shining our unique light in this cosmic play. You've got this!

Unveiling the Unseen Path

Throughout this book, we've been on a journey of unpacking the reality we were conditioned into and granting ourselves permission to create a brand-new path from within and let it shine in the world. So no need to conform to the dull status quo or exhaust ourselves fighting against the system. We're stepping into our own unique groove!

Now let's talk about humility, my friend. It's about embracing the fact that there's so much more out there that we might not even be aware of yet. It's like untangling the conditioning we soaked up in school and realizing there's a much grander reality waiting for us.

When we approach life with humility, we open up space for the magic to unfold. Our inner wisdom and desires can find their way to the surface, even when we're not entirely sure of what they are. And you know what? That's absolutely okay!

Take my client in her late fifties, for example. She retired and noticed that all her pals were busy with grandkids and family life. But she knew she needed a different journey. So, instead, she ventured into the woods, lying on the forest floor, and discovered the calling for sound healing. She might not know exactly where it'll lead, but she's breaking free from generations of family dysfunction, unleashing her true potential!

When everyone stays stuck in the same roles, nothing changes. But we're all about shaking things up and embracing the unseen path!

Your Passion is Your Soul Purpose

Hey there, dream chasers! Here's the big secret: your passions and dreams are the key to your soul purpose. Picture yourself at the end of your life, going through a life review. You wouldn't want to regret dropping the ball on your dreams, right?

So let's focus on those passions and dreams, and they'll lead us on a journey of purpose. Sometimes, the bigger picture might not be clear right away. Just like me, starting as a teen with a quirky interest in human origins and human rights, only to find my passion for evolution and freedom blending together beautifully now!

I recently spoke to someone wanting to bring animals into their office for professional work. Worried about people not taking it seriously, my advice was simple: go for it and see what happens! Animals can be part of our teams and support systems.

We need to trust the process and dare to step outside our comfort zone, away from the little box we're afraid to leave. Say our soul purpose is in the healing arts. What innate healing modalities do we possess that we want to offer to the world? It takes courage, as there's no certification or prepackaged formula, but trust in yourself and let your unique soul wisdom shine through!

And here's the icing on the cake—the proof's in the pudding! When you see the amazing results in the people you're helping, embrace humility and acknowledge that you have something incredible to offer humanity.

Are you holding onto a mind-blowing vision that feels like it's on a whole other level? Excellent! That's your soul's secret plan for this life! How cool is that?

Get ready to trust the cosmic forces, 'cause they're all in cahoots to make your grand vision a reality! It's like a cosmic conspiracy for the betterment of humanity. How epic is that?

When the time is right to unleash your soul's master plan, get ready for some cosmic decluttering! Anything that doesn't align with your mission will start falling away like confetti!

Sure, deconstruction can be a bit nerve-wracking but, remember, your soul is on a mission, and nothing can stop it! So buckle up, enjoy the wild ride, and let go of what no longer serves you. Embrace the adventure, and let the universe work its magic!

Don't hold back. Let that magical thing inside you come to life and serve the world with all your soul's power! You've got this!

Something is Knocking at Your Door

Guess what, there's something knocking at your door, and it won't take no for an answer! It's your soul purpose, ready to reveal itself and lead you on an incredible journey.

Around the age of thirty-three, things really get cookin'! You've had enough time to build your ego and identity, and now it's time to unfold your unique mission.

One common soul purpose I see in my clients is personal healing and transformation. It's like building a cleaner, more coherent template that positively impacts the whole unified field. Rockin' past our challenges is what qualifies us to help others!

Just look at Eckhart Tolle, once a neurotic professor lost in his head, now a major media figure able to reach those brainy types not willing to listen to anything woo woo. Back when his teachings didn't have much reach, he turned up the gas and asked for help. And guess what? Magic happened! Now he's inspiring people everywhere!

You can totally do it too, staying grounded and true to your purpose. And you know what the ultimate goal of soul purpose is? It's all about greater harmony, balance, and love. So let's step into that flow and spread the good vibes!

Align With Your Soul Purpose

Ready to align with your soul purpose and embark on an epic adventure?

Okay, let's break it down! So, thanks to all that cultural programming, we might not even know what we truly want or what incredible things we're capable of. But fear not! We're about to defy convention and tradition like the trailblazers we are!

But hold on, you'll need some cool tools to navigate this wild ride. Let's recap:

1. Self-Awareness: Mindfulness is the key to unlocking your potential. Mirror, mirror on the wall, who's the most aware of them all? You, of course!

2. Psychic Hygiene: Ever wanted to be like a clean-energy superhero? Well, learn to breathe and clear out those energy centers, and you'll be shining bright like a polished

diamond. Who needs heavy baggage when you can feel light and free?

3. Setting Boundaries: Time to be real and honest about what you really want. Wave goodbye to toxic situations and dance moves in the victim-perpetrator-rescuer triangle. You're too fabulous for that drama!

4. Shadow Work: Time to dive deep within and release those trapped emotions, trauma, and lost fragments of self. Get ready to level up and stop repeating the same old stories. Break free like a boss!

5. Leaps of Faith: Forget about walking, we're taking leaps of faith here! Buckle up and catapult yourself to unimaginable places. You're an expression of Source, baby, and that means you're a super creator.

Chapter Fourteen
SURRENDER

Welcome to the final chapter, my fellow soul travelers! This is no ordinary bookend—it's a magical bridge that takes us into the future and beyond. So, after using all our awesome tools, it's time for a little cosmic handoff to our Greater Self.

Let's loosen our grip a bit, shall we? If we hold on too tight or try to force things, we might accidentally slam the door on the very things we desire. If we release our attachments and surrender to the flow, we'll make room for some amazing cosmic surprises!

Let's also drop the baggage from the past. Seriously, who needs that old stuff weighing us down? Instead, let's embrace the joy of being our most authentic and radiant selves.

We're in a special cosmic era where endless possibilities await us all. It's not just a select few soaring to new heights—it's all of us on this epic journey.

Embracing Humility: Unveiling Hidden Paths to Infinite Possibilities!

Humility is like unwrapping a surprise gift, revealing the potential for something even greater in our lives. When we approach life with curiosity and openness rather than judgment, we open ourselves to new frequencies and possibilities beyond our imagination.

As we humbly shed our old skins and let go of limiting beliefs, a magnificent transformation takes place within us. We begin to witness the emergence of a more beautiful and authentic version of ourselves.

In my journey and working with clients all around the world, I've seen the power of humility, and it's reassuring to know we're not alone on this path of growth. Some souls embrace the role of trailblazers, making way for others to follow. As they pave the way, the journey becomes easier for those who walk behind.

The impact of this work is profound, as it liberates us from age-old polarities and allows us to transcend the struggles of humanity. Through this process, we break free from recurring dramas, and a world of infinite possibilities unfolds before us.

Surrendering to Your Divine Will

In the enchanting realm of surrender, we encounter a powerful mantra: "I surrender to my divine will." But what does that mean?

Sure, flexing our free will can be exhilarating, breaking away from programmed choices and conventions. Yet surrendering to our soul's purpose and plan takes us on a profound journey.

Picture it as the ultimate rubber-meets-the-road experience. Sure, we can wish and want all day long but, if our desires clash with our soul's plan for this lifetime, we may find ourselves entangled in unnecessary suffering.

Those who resonate with my messages are often coded to break out of societal norms. This courageous path involves deconstructing the life they once thought they wanted. Lo and behold, making space for the life that truly emerges can bring us profound grace!

In this delightful dance of surrender, we learn to listen to our bodies. Fear has taught them to tense up and contract, but surrendering to divine will calls for a different tune. We tune into trusting thoughts, expand our field, and open up our heart—all while letting go of that tug-of-war rope. Seriously, let go of the rope!

This beautiful shift propels us to an expansive state, where energy flows freely, creating a sense of inner peace and calm. The periods of blissful surrender grow longer, and we discover that we can truly live without constant hustling and bustling.

Oh, we'll come to realize just how delightfully neurotic we all can be! Fear may try to tell us tall tales, but we'll stand firm, stopping those projections of future horrors in their tracks.

The transformation isn't an easy-breezy spiritual bypass on a fluffy cloud. It takes work and, yes, we might face fear, anger, and sadness while bidding farewell to the old self. But the rewards of this journey far outweigh the drudgery of transactional work we don't enjoy, where we sacrifice our essence for the illusion of security.

You won't find a grand roadmap laid out before you. Instead, you'll see a few steps ahead and embark on your path without absolute guarantees. But trust yourself—you don't need to know every detail of the plan.

As a seasoned planner, I had to learn this lesson. Embracing the next level of embodiment meant letting go of everything I thought I knew. Accepting that I wouldn't have all the answers ahead of time. Embracing the mystery and surrendering to something greater than myself.

Shifting Means Shaking Things Up

As we shift, things might start to feel a bit wonky within the groups and organizations we used to resonate with. No worries, it just means we're upgrading our operating systems! So get ready to let go and walk away without taking it personally.

On this path, you'll notice that the real MVPs are the people growing and evolving right alongside you. They'll be the cheerleaders, while the critics might not be on a growth journey themselves—they're just trying to drag you down with their negativity. But guess what? You've got this!

It's crucial not to take their fear projections personally. Instead, let's minimize the trigger response and keep our focus on our newly-hatched journey of self-discovery and realization. It's like being a baseball player at the plate—sure, there's noise from the stands, but we tune in to the supportive voice within saying, "You got this, buddy!"

Think back to the times you excelled. Remember that zone where everything flowed effortlessly? Well, this journey is a bit like that! Instead of struggling and overthinking, we're going to let go and let our greater intelligence take the wheel.

Consider the journey to rediscover your Truer Self as a test of initiation—a chance to trust and surrender to a whole new level of awesomeness!

That's a Wrap! Time for a Recap

Hey there, amazing reader! Congratulations on completing this incredible journey of love and self-discovery! I hope you had a blast and found some real gems that have sprinkled a little magic in your life.

Surrender

Throughout this book, we're been on a love-filled adventure, exploring the power of positive intentions, trusting our intuition, and riding the waves of the Law of Vibration. You're facing your inner skeptic and critic like a boss, saying, "Bye-bye self-doubt, hello self-compassion!" High five to you!

Mindfulness is your BFF, helping you stay present so you can rock every situation with love and compassion. How awesome is that? And with your supercharged free will, you're taking charge of your life like a champ, creating a reality that's totally YOU-nique. Way to go!

And let's not forget the Law of Attraction. You're becoming a love magnet, attracting joy and amazing connections like confetti. You've got the love glow! You're rewriting your story with love leading the way, creating a new and empowering reality—you're like a love superhero!

By practicing psychic hygiene and embracing self-sovereignty, you've found the secret to balance and inner peace. Setting those healthy boundaries has been a game-changer, nurturing loving relationships and protecting your precious energy.

Exploring your soul purpose and passions has unlocked your true potential. And, by surrendering to divine will and letting go of attachments, you're flowing effortlessly with life, embracing new possibilities with open arms. Love's got your back!

As you wrap up this adventure, know that love isn't just a concept—it's a magical force that guides you to growth, healing, and unity. You've got that love sparkle!

So, my love-filled friend, keep on truckin' with mindfulness, trust, and self-compassion as the keys to unlock more of your deepest truth. Embrace love as your foundation, and watch your life light up like fireworks!

Epilogue: Love Is the Foundation – Embracing the Power Within

As we reach the end of this love-filled journey, I am filled with excitement for the pivotal time in human history we find ourselves in. The world is changing rapidly, and new possibilities are opening up before us like twinkling stars in the night sky. It's a time of disclosure, where the reality of non-terrestrial life is unfolding in real-time.

Amidst the awe and wonder of this cosmic revelation, we may encounter a few more bumps in the road as we navigate through the unknown. But fear not, for love will be our guiding light, leading us towards unity, understanding, and compassion.

In this transformative era, let us continue to embrace love as our ultimate foundation. With mindfulness, trust, and self-compassion as our allies, we can face any challenge with grace and resilience.

As we move forward, carrying the love sparkle in our hearts, may we play our part in creating a world that celebrates love in all its forms. And may the journey ahead be filled with joy and the endless possibilities that love unveils.

-

To make the journey a little easier (and way more sparkle-filled), I invite you to use my Daily Grounding and Clearing Meditation. It's changed people's lives! Head on over to my website and click on "Gift Meditation": www.multidimensionalu.com.

ABOUT THE AUTHOR

 A'sha (pronounced ay-sha) Love is the founder of Multidimensional U®, a multidimensional, multimedia company dedicated to the expansion of human consciousness. A graduate of William Smith College and Michigan Tech University, A'sha founded several environmental, restoration-focused nonprofit organizations before her metaphysical awakening catapulted her into alignment with her own greater calling.

A'sha received the 2021 Excellence in Education Award from the Global Forum for Education & Learning. She is a contributing author to the USA Today best-selling book, *"Luminary Leadership: How Top Entrepreneurs Lead In Business & In Life"*.

Since 2012, A'sha has designed and facilitated experiential programs to support people as they awaken to a greater multidimensional reality and engage with the alchemy of personal transformation.

Currently enjoying the rural charm of Eastern Oklahoma, she travels, as called, to conduct multidimensional field work to restore evolutionary pathways for all in this corner of the Multiverse.

Book Description

Harness the untapped power of your consciousness to become the person you want to be!

Drawing on ancient wisdom and modern science, *Love is the Foundation* reveals the incredible potential of your own consciousness to shape the world around you.

In the book, you will learn:

- Mind-opening ideas and techniques that will empower you to transform your life in profound ways.
- Practical exercises and real-world examples to help you tap into the power of your thoughts, beliefs, and emotions to create the reality you desire.
- How expanding your consciousness can be used for a variety of purposes, including manifesting abundance, healing your body, and cultivating a deeper sense of inner peace.

With insights from A'sha Love, leading expert in the field of mindfulness and personal transformation, this is a must-read for anyone seeking to unlock their full potential and live their best life.

If you're ready to take control of your reality and unleash your true potential, this book is for you.

www.ingramcontent.com/pod-product-compliance
Lightning Source LLC
Chambersburg PA
CBHW061738070526
44585CB00024B/2720